PENGUIN BOOKS

THE WINDSOR YEARS

The late Lord Kinross (Patrick Balfour) was well known on both sides of the Atlantic as an author, journalist, and broadcaster. He contributed articles to *The New Yorker, Punch, Vogue, The Queen,* and other periodicals, and he served on the editorial staffs of various newspapers. Many of his books dealt with the Middle East, and he also wrote on social customs and attitudes in the United States and Great Britain. Among his books are *Within the Taurus: A Journey in Asiatic Turkey*; *Europa Minor: Journeys in Coastal Turkey*; *Ataturk*; *Portrait of Greece*; *Portrait of Egypt*; and *The Innocents at Home: A Visit to the U.S.A.*

D1303058

The Windsor Years

THE LIFE OF EDWARD, AS PRINCE OF WALES, KING, AND DUKE OF WINDSOR

Text by
Lord Kinross
Photographs selected by the Editors

PENGUIN BOOKS

Penguin Books Ltd, Harmondsworth,
Middlesex, England
Penguin Books, 625 Madison Avenue,
New York, New York 10022, U.S.A.
Penguin Books Australia Ltd, Ringwood,
Victoria, Australia
Penguin Books Canada Limited, 2801 John Street,
Markham, Ontario, Canada L3R 1B4
Penguin Books (N.Z.) Ltd, 182–190 Wairau Road,
Auckland 10, New Zealand

First published in the United States of America by
The Viking Press (A Studio Book) 1967
First published in Canada by
The Macmillan Company of Canada Limited 1967
Published in Penguin Books 1980

LIBRARY OF CONGRESS CATALOGING IN PUBLICATION DATA
Kinross, John Patrick Douglas Balfour, Baron, 1904–1976.
The Windsor years.
Reprint of the 1967 ed. published by The Viking Press,
New York.
Includes index.
1. Edward VIII, King of Great Britain, 1894–1972.
2. Great Britain—History—20th century. 3. Great
Britain—Kings and rulers—Biography. I. Title.
[DA580.K5 1980] 941.084′092′4 [B] 79–21619
ISBN 0 14 00.5527 4

Printed in the United States of America by
The Murray Printing Company, Westford, Massachusetts
Set in Baskerville

May 1894. _George_

Chapter
I

On Midsummer Eve, 1894, at White Lodge in Richmond Park on the outskirts of London, a son was born to the Duke of York and his Duchess, the former Princess Mary of Teck. His birth was an event of significance, as a grandson to the Prince of Wales, the future King Edward VII, and as a great-grandson to Queen Victoria, now in the fifty-eighth year of her reign. It meant that, for the first time in English history, the male succession to the Throne was ensured, during the lifetime of a reigning sovereign, through three direct living descendants.

The Duke of York, the future King George V, pronounced the baby a "sweet little boy." The Cabinet Minister in attendance, Mr. Asquith, announced his safe delivery by telegram to Queen Victoria at Windsor Castle and to the Prince of Wales, who, with his Princess, Alexandra of Denmark, was giving a ball in celebration of the Ascot Races, in a neo-classical temple near by. The Prince at once stopped the band, proclaimed the birth of his first grandson, and proposed a toast to him, which was drunk by the guests in champagne.

Queen Victoria, driving over to tea at White Lodge a day or so later, voted him "a fine strong-looking child," but observed that his mouth was too large. His own mother, the future Queen Mary, wrote of her first-born, the future Prince Charming, that he was "exactly what I looked like as a baby, consequently *plain!* This is a pity and rather disturbs me."

Meanwhile, the morrow of his birth being a Sunday, and a fine one, loyal clergymen made it an occasion for sermons, for which Shakespeare provided a text: "Now is the winter of our discontent made glorious summer by this son

The Duke and Duchess of York with Prince Edward, born June 23, 1894.

of York." Less loyal, less content, was the voice of the Radical leader, Keir Hardie, who spoke in Parliament against an address of congratulation to the Queen on the birth of her great-grandson. "From his childhood," he ventured to prophesy, "this boy will be surrounded by sycophants and flatterers by the score, and will be taught to believe himself as of a superior creation. A line will be drawn between him and the people he might be called to rule over. In due course, following the precedent which has already been set, he will be sent on a tour round the world, and probably rumours of a morganatic marriage will follow, and the end of it will be that the country will be called upon to pay the bill." His words provoked loud cries of protest.

The boy meanwhile was christened in the presence of Queen Victoria, swaddled in a lace robe copied from her wedding veil, and anointed with Jordan water from a golden bowl, used at such ceremonies since the reign of Edward VI. Afterwards "the dear fine baby," as the Queen now described him, was photographed on her lap in a family group of the four generations, which was distributed throughout Britain and the Empire.

She insisted that he be given the name of Albert, thus perpetuating the memory of her lamented husband, the Prince Consort; also that of her more lately lamented grandson, the Duke of Clarence, who had been heir to his father, the Prince of Wales, until his untimely death, two years before, at the age of twenty-eight. He had been engaged to Princess "May," whom Queen Victoria had earmarked as a future Queen of England, and who had thus, after a decent interval, married the Duke of York instead. The name of Edward, however, that of the Prince of Wales and of seven English kings before him, was allowed to take precedence, and the baby embarked upon life as Prince Edward Albert Christian George Andrew Patrick David. Christian was the name of the King of Denmark, the father of the Princess of Wales; the last four names were those of the patron saints of England, Scotland, Ireland, and Wales, and it was as David that the Prince became known in his family circle.

It was a circle, as time was to reveal to him, fraught with conflicting personal relationships. The Queen, now also Empress of India, was its matriarch, a remote but still formidable figure, presiding over her numerous progeny as she presided over an Empire which, having doubled in size since she came to the Throne, covered a quarter of the globe. Three years after the birth of Prince Edward she celebrated, amid the plaudits of a nation in its hey-day and of far-flung dominions still in their early youth, the Diamond Jubilee of a reign which had started in 1837. She was to see the turn of the century and to die, when the Prince was six years old, at the age of eighty-one.

An early photograph of Queen Victoria with Prince Albert.

A shoulder-high ride—Princess Alexandra carries her son Prince George, who was later to be Duke of York and King George V. He was born in 1865.

The future King Edward VII as Prince of Wales, with his bride, Princess Alexandra, daughter of King Christian IX of Denmark, and Queen Victoria, his mother.

LEFT: Prince George as a young man (right) with his elder brother, Prince Albert Victor, later Duke of Clarence. Prince George became heir to the throne when his brother died at the age of twenty-eight. RIGHT: Princess Mary of Teck (above) and Prince George (below), whom she was to marry. OPPOSITE: Mary and George, who became the Duke and Duchess of York after their wedding, with Queen Victoria, the Duke's grandmother.

Prince Edward (now the Duke of Windsor) was born to the Duke and Duchess of York on June 23, 1894. OPPOSITE: Four generations and four monarchs: the Queen holds her great-grandson, Prince Edward, later King Edward VIII, while his father, the Duke of York, later George V, and his grandfather, later King Edward VII, stand in the background.

OVERLEAF: Prince Edward by a lily pond, arrayed in the frills and ribbons of a Victorian toddler's dress.

BELOW AND RIGHT: As if foreshadowing his future career, the young prince carries his flag like a rifle, and stands to attention in a sailor's uniform.

ABOVE: A charming portrait of Prince Edward with his mother. LEFT: The infant prince takes a royal carriage ride, his horses showing their paces across the nursery.

19

For the Diamond Jubilee of Queen Victoria in 1887 the shipping fleets at anchor
are decked in flags (LEFT) and the Queen tours London (ABOVE), shaded by a para-
sol, while some spectators find a grandstand view from the National Gallery roof.

ABOVE: The Queen in a family group. Front left to right: Leopold of Battenberg, Princess Marie Louise, Prince Edward (now Duke of Windsor), The Duchess of York (later Queen Mary), Princess Victoria of York, Margaret of Connaught (standing), Alexander of Battenberg (sitting on the ground), Prince Albert (later George VI) (standing), The Duke of York (later George V) (standing), Queen Victoria, Arthur of Connaught (standing), Duchess of Connaught, Patricia of Connaught (sitting on the ground), Princess Beatrice of Battenberg, Ena of Battenberg (standing), Helena Victoria of Schleswig-Holstein, Maurice of Battenberg.

The Queen in 1900 poses with her great-grandchildren Prince Albert, Princess Mary, Prince Edward, and Prince Henry in his swaddling clothes. This is one of the last pictures of Queen Victoria. January 1901 saw the end of her sixty-four-year reign and the accession of her son as King Edward VII.

As a widow she came seldom to London, visiting Buckingham Palace for brief periods only, two or three times each year, and living largely in the seclusion of Windsor Castle, surrounded by the possessions of a lifetime and frequented by a varying concourse of relatives, for the most part Germanic in origin. The Castle, a historic medieval pile suitably Victorianized, brooded over the small town of Windsor. Its towers and battlements surveyed a great Royal Park and beyond it a gentle English landscape, refreshed by the waters of the meandering Thames.

Here, as he grew from babyhood to childhood, Prince Edward used to be taken to visit his "Gan-Gan," often with his brother Prince Albert, born eighteen months after him on the mournful anniversary of the Prince Consort's death. He was always intimidated and often reduced to tears by her forbidding presence and that of the fierce-looking Indian retainers whom she gathered around her. This displeased his great-grandmother, who would vent her irritation on the children's nurse, Mrs. Bill. ("You had to mind your step with Queen Victoria," she would afterwards recall.) It was recalled by Prince Edward, however, that once, in a more relaxed and even playful mood, he tried to heave the Queen out of her chair, crying to her "Get up, Gan-Gan!" and commanding the bearded Indian, "Man, pull it!"

By the end of her long reign Queen Victoria had established the British monarchy, in the hearts and minds of its subjects, on a new and it seemed unshakeable basis. She invested the Crown, and by reflection the Empire, with a mystique tinged by the aura of divinity. She set, in her personal life, high moral standards to serve as an example to her people—the growing middle class on which the Empire's prosperity rested. As few sovereigns had been before her, Queen Victoria was the incarnation of respectability, social propriety, and God-fearing morality.

The Prince of Wales, now in his fifties and soon to be King Edward VII, presented a personal image noticeably different from that of the Queen. Debarred by her, despite his acknowledged ability, from any share in the responsibilities of State, he spent his life, as she saw it, in "one whirl of amusement." His princely pleasures were those of the race-course, the card-room, the dinner table, and the alcove, for he was gay and sporting, and free-and-easy in his relationships with women. Socially he and his Princess, a woman of notable beauty and grace, had become the leaders of a fashionable world, the sophisticated *élite* of the new generation which was emerging from the Victorian Age to greet the twentieth century. It reacted with tolerance to such lapses by the Prince of Wales as appalled Queen Victoria—his implication in a society divorce case, his presence at the baccarat table at Tranby Croft, when a Scottish baronet was found to be cheating.

To the young Prince Edward his grandfather seemed, as he was later to remember him, "bathed in perpetual sunlight." "Few men," he wrote, "could match his vitality, his sheer *joie de vivre*." He remembered him especially "presiding over a well-laden table" or making gallant gestures towards beautiful women. A mutual affection, based on certain affinities of temperament, soon grew up between them, surviving a recorded incident at table when the older Edward reproved the younger for an interruption, to be greeted afterwards with the retort: "It doesn't matter now, Grandfather. There was a slug in your salad. But you've eaten it." Queen Victoria might not have been amused. The Prince of Wales was. Prince Edward was always at ease with him, as with one of his own age. Once, opening the door to a visitor, he called out: "Come in. There's nobody here . . . nobody that matters. Only Grandpa."

When the grandparents became King and Queen, the parents were dispatched on a long tour of the Empire, as Duke and Duchess of Cornwall, and confided the children to their care. Queen Alexandra was a warm-hearted, indulgent woman, and between them she and King Edward exercised to the full the grandparental privilege of spoiling them. At Sandringham, the sumptuous mock-Tudor mansion in Norfolk around which the King had developed a sporting estate renowned for its lavish profusion of game birds, they encouraged the young Princes in their play at the expense of their lessons, waving the governess away with the reassurance, "It's all right. Let the children stay with us a little longer. We shall send them upstairs presently." Even when the parents were at home, the grandparents took pleasure in subverting their discipline, sending the children home late from a gay visit to the "Big House," to face a summons to the paternal study and royal reproof from their father, watch in hand.

Home, for the boys, meant a smaller house and a sterner regime. York Cottage, where the family lived, was a mere bachelor's cottage, originally built in the Sandringham grounds as an overflow for guests, and given to the Duke as a wedding present by his father, whose addiction to shooting he shared. The children, who increased in number as the years went by, were confined to two small rooms on the top floor, the day and night nurseries, where they lived and slept in congested seclusion. At Frogmore, a more commodious house in Windsor Great Park, where they spent part of the summer, their attic quarters nevertheless grew so stuffy that the roof above them, built from the best quality lead, had periodically to be sprayed with water to cool it and enable the children to breathe freely.

Their days were passed in relative seclusion. They saw little of their father, though the aura of his strict presence pervaded the house. They saw only a little

Young Prince Edward in a sailor suit.

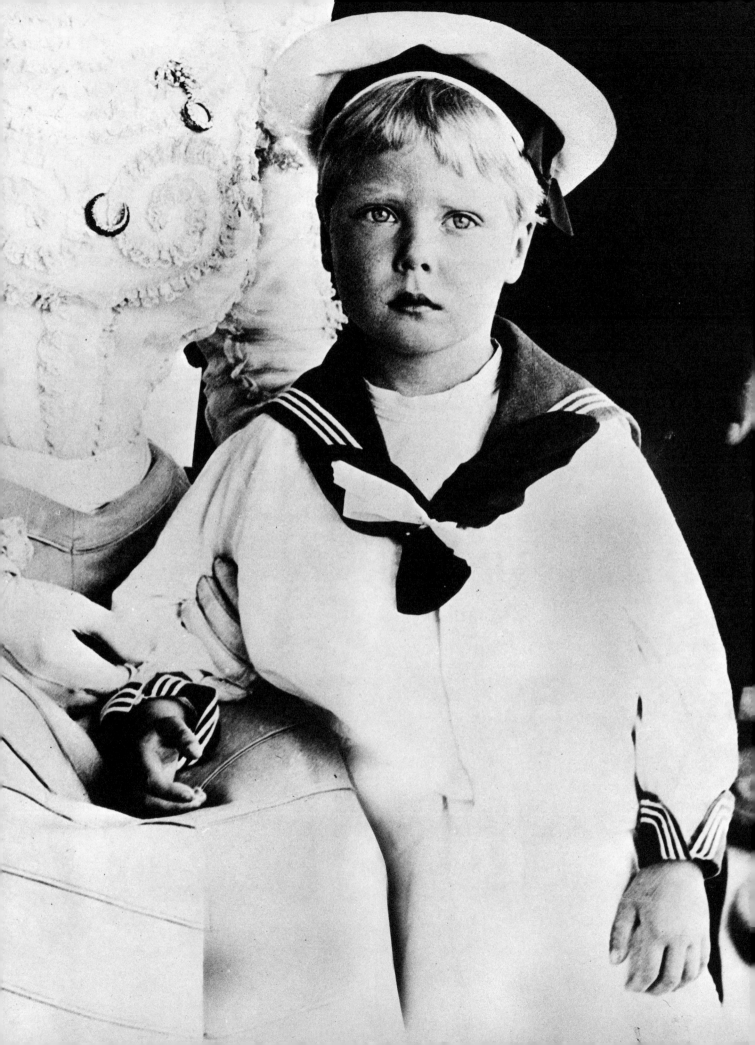

more of their mother, whom they were taken to visit each evening as she relaxed in her cosy, brightly furnished boudoir. A woman of refinement and culture, she would read and talk to them and sometimes teach them songs at the piano, through the last precious hour of the children's day. Thus there grew up between the young Prince and his mother a relationship which was fond but which never grew intimate. For she did not wholly understand the minds and ways of children, and was moreover wholly dedicated to the service of her husband, both as wife and as Consort. As Queen she once remarked of her sons, "I have always to remember that their father is also their King."

Four royal brothers in Scotland. Left to right: Prince Henry, Prince Albert, Prince George, and Prince Edward—known among themselves as Harry, Bertie, George, and David. At this time the fifth brother, John, was still an infant, and he died at the age of fourteen. OPPOSITE: Grouse-shooting on the moors near Balmoral.

As Duke of York, he had devoted his career to the Royal Navy. This "Senior Service" of the British Raj had inspired him with all that patriotic loyalty and devotion to duty which was admirably to fit him for kingship, as George V, through a period of war and unrest. "He had," as his son afterwards put it, "the Victorian's sense of probity, moral responsibility, and love of domesticity." But his naval background meant that he imposed upon the home much of the punctilio and discipline of the ward-room and the quarter-deck: "The laws of behaviour as revealed to a small boy tended to be ruled by a vast preponderance of 'don'ts.'"

The York family migrated, with the seasonal regularity of birds, between their homes of York Cottage, Frogmore, and Abergeldie in the grounds of Balmoral—the Gothic castle, blazing with tartan upholstery and ringing with the music of bagpipes, which Queen Victoria and Prince Albert had erected amid the moors and glens of the Scottish highlands. In these various royal houses the children led lives curiously isolated, by their elevated status, from children of their own age. Nor was this remedied when Prince Edward and his brother Albert reached the age for serious schooling. For their father was of a conservative stamp and believed that what had been good enough for himself was still good enough, thirty years later, for his sons. Instead of being sent to a preparatory boarding-school, like most boys of their age and generation, they were to be taught at home by a tutor until old enough to go into the Navy, as he himself had been.

The tutor he selected for them was a man of his own generation, Henry Hansell. A typical English schoolmaster, tweeded and pipe-smoking, of the muscular-Christian breed, he was proficient in games and to a lesser extent in classical and historical scholarship. He soon transformed the former nursery into a convincing replica of a classroom at a preparatory school, with standard school desks, blackboards, and maps on the walls, and here the two boys settled down to a methodical routine of primary studies. Prince Edward's progress was slow. For this his mother blamed Mr. Hansell, who proved indeed to be a man of pedestrian mind, with few positive views upon anything and little talent for inspiring curiosity in the young.

Mr. Hansell himself, as the boys grew older, seemed aware of his own limitations, and periodically urged that Prince Edward would be better able to hold his own in a naval academy if grounded at a preparatory school. But his father would not hear of so unprecedented a step, and blamed the boy's own natural dumbness for the delay in his progress. Meanwhile Prince Edward had been removed from the nursery to the charge of a personal footman named Finch, a young and stalwart personality, respectful but in no way servile, who was to remain in his service, first as valet, then as butler, for the rest of his life, and whose company he found more rewarding than that of his tutor.

Queen Victoria died, and an age of English history ended, early in 1901. Prince Edward was then six-and-a-half years old. He was taken to the funeral services in St. George's Chapel at Windsor and to the interment beside the Prince Consort in the royal mausoleum at Frogmore. But at so early an age he was only aware, as he afterwards described it, of "the piercing cold, the interminable waits, and of feeling very lost among scores of grown-up relatives—solemn princes in varied uniforms and princesses sobbing behind heavy *crêpe* veils!"

Eighteen months later his grandfather and grandmother were crowned King Edward VII and Queen Alexandra in Westminster Abbey. The two small Princes watched the ceremony from a box reserved for princesses, dressed in kilts of the Balmoral tartan and attended by Mr. Hansell and Finch. They fidgeted and whispered as their father did homage to their grandfather as King, and broke into suppressed giggles when one of their great-aunts dropped her embossed Order of Service with a clatter over the edge of the box into a gold vessel below. Their father and mother were now Prince and Princess of Wales, and Prince Edward of Wales moved up one stage nearer to his fateful destiny as King of Great Britain and Ireland and the British Dominions beyond the Seas, and Emperor of India.

King Edward VII, after his coronation in 1902.

28

King Edward with a hunting party, including the exiled King Manuel of Portugal.

A few years later. The King and Queen leave Windsor Castle for a day at Ascot.

The King's son, George (then Prince of Wales and heir to the throne), sits next to the driver in the first Rolls-Royce.

Chapter
II

"The Navy will teach David all he needs to know." Such was the dictum of the new heir to the Throne on the education of his son and his preparation for the duties of kingship. Deriving from his own restricted experience, it ignored the important fact that he himself, as Duke of York, had been a second son, for whom the naval profession was traditionally regarded as suitable, with an elder brother, the Duke of Clarence, whose education was geared a shade closer to wider and graver responsibilities.

Thus in his thirteenth year, still small in stature and in many ways young for his age, Prince Edward of Wales left, in the company of his father and in floods of tears, for Osborne, a former seaside residence of Queen Victoria, built in the style of an Italianate villa. Its crumbling stables had now been converted into a preparatory academy for naval cadets, with a central hall called Nelson, prominently inscribed with the Admiral's famous motto, "There is nothing the Navy cannot do." In this "naval mill" Prince Edward was to learn not geography, history, and modern languages, for which he showed some aptitude, but a smattering of mathematics, navigation, science, and engineering, together with such accomplishments as tying knots, splicing ropes, reading signals, boxing the compass, and sailing a cutter.

He was above all thrown together for the first time with boys of his own age—boys especially vetted by a selection committee for those qualities of efficiency, sportsmanship, toughness, and *esprit de corps* likely to make of them good "officer material" at sea. His father had insisted that he be treated on a level with the other boys. He was known to them as Edward ("Edward what?" "Just Edward"), but they cut him down to his natural size by coining for him the nickname of "Sardines," as a schoolboy antithesis to Wales. Within a day or two of his arrival he was anointed by a gang of senior boys with a bottle of red ink, poured over his all too fair hair. Later, as a reminder of the fate of his forebear

Prince Edward, out running with the cadets from Osborne, turns toward the camera.

The Queen, accompanied by Princess Victoria, peers over the side of her carriage to watch the repair of a puncture which delayed them in Holborn Circus, London. OPPOSITE: The King with his son George and grandson Edward.

Charles I, he was "guillotined," by the banging down on his neck of an open classroom window.

Otherwise he soon adapted himself to the normal hazards of cadet life—to the dormitory rigours of iron bed, sea chest, and early morning cold showers, to the fierce, gregarious rivalries and feuds of an unfamiliar community life. After two years he was transferred, for the second spell of his naval shore training, to the more commodious college of Dartmouth, a series of red-brick buildings on a Devon hillside overlooking the River Dart, where he enjoyed better food—including Devonshire cream—and a little more freedom. Here he made a few friends and began to feel that he was at last growing up.

Meanwhile, early in his second year at Dartmouth, the pattern of the Prince's life was interrupted by the death of his grandfather, King Edward VII, after a reign of only nine years. The Prince and his brother first learned of this mournful event early on a May morning through the sight, from their bedroom window in Marlborough House, of the Royal Standard flying at half-mast over Buckingham Palace—an error at once peremptorily corrected by their father on the established principle, "The King is dead. Long live the King." Prince Edward, now by inheritance Duke of Cornwall, drove in a State coach with his mother and sister in the funeral procession through London to Paddington station, then walked in his naval uniform behind his father, now King George V, up the hill to the interment at Windsor, followed throughout by a cortège which included nine other reigning monarchs.

Then he returned to Dartmouth, where his studies were supplemented by a course in civics, designed, together with a more attentive study of the newspapers, to awaken in him some understanding of the mysteries of statecraft and politics. This was a timely innovation, at a moment when Radical forces in Britain had put a Liberal government in power. It had embarked upon a policy of swift social change, creating immediate new problems for the monarchy and within a generation transforming much of the structure of Britain. The death of King Edward VII was indeed the beginning of the end of an era.

Soon after it, on the Prince's sixteenth birthday, his father created him Prince of Wales. Next day he was confirmed by the Archbishop of Canterbury in the private chapel at Windsor Castle, an initial preparation for his ultimate role as Defender of the Faith. A year later, before the coronation of his father and mother as King George V and Queen Mary in Westminster Abbey, he was invested at Windsor Castle with the Order of the Garter, that ancient order of English chivalry once praised by a British statesman on the grounds that there was "no damned merit" about it. "I wore," the Prince recalled afterwards, "a cloth-of-silver costume, white stockings and white satin slippers with red heels, and a sword in a red velvet scabbard hung at my side."

The funeral procession for King Edward VII in 1910 at Windsor. Young Edward (who had become the Duke of Cornwall on his father's accession) walks with his brother behind the coffin of his grandfather. Among the dignitaries are King Edward's brother, the Duke of Connaught; King Edward's son-in-law, the Duke of Fife; and Queen Mary's three brothers, Prince Adolphus of Teck, Prince Francis of Teck, and Lord Athlone. Prince Louis Alexander of Battenberg (later Marquess of Milford Haven), and Prince Max of Baden were also present at the funeral. BELOW: King George V is accompanied by eight reigning sovereigns, including the Kaiser Wilhelm II, the Kings of Belgium, Denmark, Greece, Norway, Portugal, and Spain, and Czar Ferdinand of Bulgaria. Emperor Franz Josef of Austria was represented by the Archduke Franz Ferdinand, Czar Nicholas II of Russia by his brother the Grand Duke Michael Alexandrovitch, and the King of Italy by the Duke of Aosta. Theodore Roosevelt (at extreme right) was one of the many special ambassadors who attended the funeral.

In this costume, with the blue riband and star of the Order, he took part in the coronation ceremony, kneeling at his father's feet to do homage with the words "I Edward, Prince of Wales, do become your liege man of life and limb, and of earthly worship; and faith and truth I will bear unto you, to live and die, against all manner of folks. So help me God." The King wrote afterwards in his diary, "I nearly broke down when dear David came to do homage to me, as it reminded me so much when I did the same thing to beloved Papa, he did it so well. Darling May looked lovely, and it was indeed a comfort to me to have her by my side, as she has been ever to me during these last eighteen years."

Some weeks later, in a picturesque ceremony revived after a lapse of some centuries, the Prince was invested, in Caernarvon Castle, with the honours of his new Principality of Wales. Coached by the Welsh Radical leader, Lloyd George, he had to make a speech in the Welsh tongue. But this worried him less than the clothes he was expected to wear for the ceremony, "a fantastic costume," as he described it, "designed for the occasion, consisting of white satin breeches and a mantle and surcoat of purple velvet edged with ermine. . . . What would my Navy friends say if they saw me in this preposterous rig? There was a family blow-up that night; but in the end my mother, as always, smoothed things over. 'You mustn't take a mere ceremony so seriously,' she said. 'Your friends will understand that as a Prince you are obliged to do certain things that may seem a little silly.' "

The ceremony, before a crowd of ten thousand, with Winston Churchill, as Home Secretary, eloquently proclaiming the young Prince's titles, left him with the conviction that, "while I was prepared to fulfil my role in all this pomp and ritual, I recoiled from anything that tended to set me up as a person requiring homage. Even if my father was now beginning to remind me of the obligations of my position, had he not been at pains to give me a strict and unaffected upbringing? And if my association with the village boys at Sandringham and the cadets of the Naval Colleges had done anything for me, it was to make me desperately anxious to be treated exactly like any other boy of my age." Here within him, as he reached the age of seventeen, was the Prince's first intimation of a problem which was to unsettle his life henceforward—that of a deep-rooted conflict, never wholly to be resolved, between his private and his public self.

David Lloyd George accompanied by Winston Churchill, shortly before the coronation of King George V and Queen Mary. Both statesmen were to guide and influence Edward at various times in his career. At the time of the photograph Lloyd George was Chancellor of the Exchequer and Churchill was Home Secretary.

The Prince was invested with the Order of the Garter at Windsor Castle on June 10, 1911. He had been created a Knight of the Garter in June 1910. OPPOSITE: He is shown wearing the regalia. ABOVE: King George and Queen Mary at the ceremony. BELOW: The royal party, returning from St. George's Chapel after the ceremony. They are about to enter the Tudor cottages which are now used as choristers' residences.

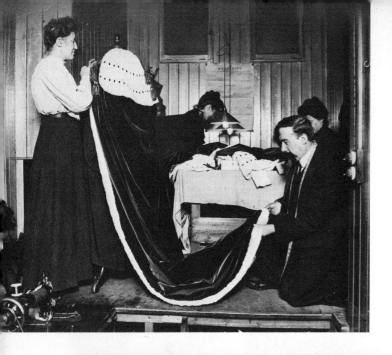

ABOVE LEFT: Before the coronation of George V on June 22, 1911, the robes are carefully inspected in the workrooms of Messrs. Ede, Son and Ravenscroft. ABOVE RIGHT: Coronation guests, decked out for the occasion.

LEFT: The Prince (wearing the Order of the Garter) and Princess Mary, in the robes they wore for the coronation of their father. OPPOSITE: The new King and Queen in full regalia.

OVERLEAF: The coronation procession of King George V passes through the streets of London.

Prince Edward was created Prince of Wales in June 1910, but the ceremony investing him with the title (at Caernarvon Castle) did not take place until July 1911. ABOVE: The Prince stands under a canopy before his father and mother, while the Home Secretary, Winston Churchill (at left), proclaims his titles. OPPOSITE: Invested with the honor of his principality, the Prince walks with the King and Queen in the procession that followed.

The Prince of Wales stands before the cheering crowds, and is then driven through the streets of Caernarvon.

LEFT: The King and Queen, Emperor and Empress of India, at the coronation Durbar in Delhi in 1911. ABOVE: Winston Churchill, the First Lord of the Admiralty, meeting the King and Queen at Portsmouth on the return of their majesties from India. OVERLEAF: The Royal train that took the King and Queen from Portsmouth to London.

Already, on account of his father's coronation, he had been removed prematurely from Dartmouth, and thus denied the coveted training course, in North American waters, which would have set the seal on his career as a cadet. Sensing his disappointment, his father now arranged for him to go to sea for a brief spell as a midshipman in the battleship H.M.S. *Hindustan*. Here he spent what he liked later to describe as the happiest days of his youth. As the most junior of the junior officers on board, he ranked, in naval slang, as a "wart," a species whose function was to fetch and carry for his seniors but otherwise make himself scarce. Forbidden by naval rules to smoke or drink, since he was under eighteen, he was nevertheless allowed a glass of port on guest nights and a cigarette when engaged on the grimy and laborious task of coaling ship.

For all this, he found the atmosphere of the warship more adult than that of the naval academies. At other tasks he did his best to learn, in three months, what the average midshipman learned in three years. The naval authorities reported of him that "throughout the whole period of his training on board he has been an extremely hard worker and has struck all those about him, high and low, as what we call a 'live thing.' " As his shipmates found, he was "not so timorous as he seemed nor as angelic as he looked." He had come at last to enjoy the Navy, and would have taken kindly to a naval career.

But in this, as in other aspirations to come, he was doomed to frustration. For his father now broke to him the news that he was to leave the service, as he himself had left it—though at a later age—on the death of his elder brother. It offered a career, the King contended, "too specialized" for the heir to the Throne. The Navy could not, after all, teach David all he needed to know. He was now, so his father informed him, to make educational trips abroad, to France and Germany; and then he was to go to Oxford University.

The prospect of travel attracted the Prince, who had always chafed at the absence of foreign languages from his educational curriculum. But the prospect of going to Oxford dismayed him. In his modest way he realized that Osborne and Dartmouth had in no way prepared him for intellectual studies. He protested to his father that he had "neither the mind nor the will for books" and that his years at a university would be wasted. "If I cannot stay in the Navy," he pleaded, "please let me go round the world and learn about the different countries and their peoples at first hand." But King George was adamant—reinforced in his attitude by Mr. Hansell, who had suggested the idea to him in the first place and had recommended his own old college, Magdalen. On learning that his tutor was the "villain of the plot," the Prince gave him a piece of his mind, using words which, as he put it, were "nobody's business."

Prince Edward aboard H.M.S. *Hindustan*, 1911.

Crowds gather on the quay outside the club of the Royal Yacht Squadron.
An early photograph of the annual sailing regatta at Cowes. BELOW: The
King on the deck of the royal yacht *Britannia,* in which he won many regatta
prizes. With him is the Master of the Household, Sir Derek Keppel.

OPPOSITE: The Prince with the Duchess of Aosta at the wedding of the exiled King Manuel II of Portugal and Princess Augusta Victoria of Hohenzollern.

ABOVE: An informal luncheon in Queen Alexandra's apartments, Sandringham. BELOW: The Queen, Princess Mary, and the Prince of Wales watch a review of the Officers' Training Corps in Windsor Great Park.

Queen Mary descends the gang-way to "step ashore" from a model of H.M.S. *Repulse* at an exhibition at Earl's Court, London. The King and Princess Mary stand at the top of the steps watching her.

Meanwhile Mr. Hansell, together with Finch, accompanied him on a four-month tour of France—the Prince's first trip abroad since a brief visit to his relatives in Denmark at the age of four. His grandfather, King Edward VII, had won the hearts of the French, becoming the architect, at a crucial moment in international relations, of the *Entente Cordiale*. Now, in its hey-day, they began to discern in this new young Prince of Wales signs of the charm and the frankness and the zest for life of the other.

In Paris he stayed with a friend of his grandfather, the Marquis de Breteuil, a bon viveur of civilized tastes with an American-born wife and two young sons a little older than their guest. They entertained the beau-monde and the intelligentsia in a fine house in the Bois de Boulogne, and enjoyed country life at a château in the Chevreuse valley, near Paris—where oddly enough the Prince was himself destined, in later life, to make his home. Now he studied French grammar and history with a bearded and tail-coated tutor named Escoffier, did a course of sightseeing in museums, churches, and châteaux so intensive as to give him twinges of cultural indigestion, acquired a taste for the pleasures of motoring in a tour across France, went on a cruise with the French Fleet in the Mediterranean, and was invested by the President of the Republic in person with the Legion of Honour.

Next year he paid two visits to Germany, where he felt more at home, speaking the language more fluently and enjoying the hospitality of German relatives who ruled over princely and grand-ducal domains in various parts of the Reich. He admired "the modesty, the perseverance, the discipline, the thoroughness, and the love of the Fatherland so typical of the German people." He met Count Zeppelin, and inspected the prototype of the airship which in a few years' time would be bombing London. He had his first taste of night life in Berlin, locking up his German tutor in his hotel bathroom to escape with his equerry into the cabarets and dance clubs of the gay, wicked city.

He paid a courtesy call on his cousin Kaiser Wilhelm II, who received him in uniform, sitting on a military saddle behind a high desk, entertained him to dinner, and, changing into another uniform, swept him off to a performance at the Opera. Afterwards the Emperor remarked of him: "A most charming, unassuming young man such as one would expect from such a family—but a young eagle, likely to play a big part in European affairs because he is far from being a pacifist."

In the Prince such foreign trips whetted an appetite for travel which was to last him all his days. They made Oxford seem "a dreary chore to be finished with the least possible effort and as quickly as possible." When Edward VII went

The Prince of Wales with the Oxford University Officers' Training Corps during manœuvres.

ABOVE: Magdalen College, Oxford. BELOW LEFT: With the famous cricketer W. G. Grace, at Magdalen, where the Prince was a student for two years before the First World War. BELOW RIGHT: Out hunting on foot, following the Magdalen and New College beagles.

up to Oxford—and later to Cambridge—as Prince of Wales, he ranked as a "nobleman," wore a specially designed cap and gown, and lived in segregation from his fellow collegians in a house of his own, where he received much of his tuition. His grandson, on the other hand, attended though he was by an equerry, Major Cadogan, and by the inevitable Mr. Hansell, ranked as a commoner, lived in a set of rooms on a staircase in Magdalen College, and generally led the ordinary life of an ordinary undergraduate.

He attended lectures in his own and other colleges, rubbing shoulders with budding Socialist students, while their comrades obligingly dispersed sightseeing crowds by pouring water over their heads from bedroom windows. Christ Church, his grandfather's more aristocratic college, salved wounded pride at his choice of Magdalen with the comment, "Of course, the Prince of Wales wants to come into contact with the ordinary Tom, Dick, and Harry—what then would be the use of his coming to Christ Church?" The Prince's great-aunt Augusta, Grand Duchess of Mecklenburg-Strelitz, expressed disapproval of the whole venture in a letter to his mother, Queen Mary: "Why is he to be an undergraduate? Surely this cannot be true. It is too democratic, and why?"

But Oxford life at this level suited the Prince well enough. "Bookish he will never be," wrote the President of Magdalen, his tutor in the humanities—much as Gladstone had remarked of his grandfather, that he "knew everything except what is written in books." He was not especially studious, though his mind was awakened by this new tutor, as the Navy had failed to awaken it, to an interest in history. In the weathered stone courtyards of his historic college, with its meadows and its medieval deer park and the tower of its chapel forever dreaming by the banks of the Cherwell, he tasted for the first time personal independence.

He enjoyed the free-and-easy social ways of his fellow-undergraduates—breakfasting with them in the Junior Common Room; hob-nobbing with them in "Gunner's," the congested little office of Gunstone, its steward, an old-timer with a rich repertoire of stories and tricks; taking wine and dessert with them after dinner in Hall on Sunday nights; making new friends and entertaining them in his own rooms to informal meals sent up from the college kitchen. He joined in the more high-spirited entertainments of bump-suppers culminating in bonfires when the college boat had bumped its way to the head of the river; conspiratorial sessions of roulette for small stakes, behind closed doors; drinking parties to celebrate twenty-first birthdays. The Prince often added to the gaiety of such evenings by playing and singing to the banjo, once exchanging it for the skirl of the bagpipe to disperse a party of rowdies demonstrating beneath his windows with an improvised tin-pan band.

Taking pleasure in sports, he played football for the Magdalen second eleven. A press photograph of an opponent bearing down on him in a college match aroused concern in high quarters for his dignity as heir apparent. But in plebeian eyes it was enhanced by his participation in so popular a national game. Cricket was too slow for his temperament, but he played tennis and bettered his golf, a game in which his progress had been arrested by his father's refusal to allow him to take lessons. He beagled with the packs of other colleges; he shot a little, from neighbouring country houses, though he never came to care for the sport as his father did.

Finally he took to riding, at first in reluctant response to his father's commands, but in time, as he gained in confidence and his horsemanship improved under his equerry's instruction, with pleasure. On his first day out hunting, the South Oxfordshire hounds, as though in his honour, killed no fewer than five foxes. Soon he was hunting regularly with one or other of the three famous packs in the neighbourhood, riding out to the outskirts of the city on his bicycle—and later, when he was allowed by his father to possess one, driving out in his car—to join his mount and proceed with the equerry to the meet of the hounds. Ironically enough the sport of riding, into which his father thus pushed him against his will, was to become, in his later youth, his favourite pastime—by now against his father's will.

Finally the Prince voluntarily enlisted as a private in the Oxford Battalion of the Officers' Training Corps, in which he rose to be a corporal, doing weekly drills and parades and twice attending the annual O.T.C. camp near Aldershot. In a mock-battle between Oxford and Cambridge he was in command of the scouts of his corps, who won distinction by detecting and discomfiting an enemy ambush. The Prince, traditionally destined as heir to the Throne to hold commissions in both services, thus added a spell of infantry training to his more thorough training as a sailor. This was followed by a brief bout of cavalry training at home, in the Life Guards.

He left Oxford in June 1914 and looked forward to a summer and autumn spent travelling abroad, in Germany and elsewhere, before joining the Grenadier Guards as an infantry officer. Meanwhile he plunged for a few weeks into the entertainments of the London season of 1914, dancing all night in the great houses whose families still ruled society. But clouds of war were gathering from the direction of Germany. On July 31 the Prince of Wales wrote in his diary, "I was reading newspapers all night, and Papa received news of Belgium's mobilization. All this is too ghastly and that we should be on the brink of war is almost incredible; I am very depressed." Three days later the German army invaded Belgium.

The Prince of Wales in the uniform of a Lieutenant of the Royal Navy, 1913.

66

Chapter III

The war, to the Prince of Wales, was a time of frustration. The world conflict brought to a head the conflict inherent within him, between private and public self. To himself he was any ordinary young Englishman of twenty, responding in a patriotic spirit to the crisis confronting his country. Like the rest of his generation he was eager to fight and ready if need be to die for the flag. But to those in authority he was the heir to the Throne, hence must not be permitted to risk his life. He was not long in making this bitter discovery.

On the night of the declaration of war, August 4, 1914, "the parents," so he recorded in his diary, emerged onto the balcony of Buckingham Palace "amid an unparalleled demonstration of patriotism." After they had retired to bed, "the people remained singing, cheering and whistling for another 3 hours, and I was lulled to sleep by their fearful shindy at 1.30." Earlier he had written, "Oh!! God; the whole thing is too big to comprehend!! Oh!! that I had a job." He hoped to be allowed to join the Navy, which was after all his first career. But the seas were alive with submarines, and the Admiralty refused to take this responsibility. His second career however was the Army and, after some delay, he was granted a commission, signed by his father, in the Grenadier Guards, with a posting to the regiment's 1st Battalion near London. "It was a happy moment for me," he wrote, "and now I am an officer in the army and am going to do active service!! I get away from this awful palace where I have had the worst weeks of my life!"

Detailed to the King's Company of six-footers, "a pygmy among giants" since he failed to make the grade by five inches, he worked hard at battalion training, took part in route marches and field exercises, practised on the rifle ranges, and under a fierce sergeant-major paraded for squad drill "on the

The Prince of Wales as a twenty-year-old Guards officer.

ABOVE: The King inspecting a detachment of the Tank Corps in England. LEFT: The Prince in the uniform of the Grenadier Guards. OPPOSITE: In France, where the Prince did his best to reach the forefront of the battle. The British troops are near Nesle, on the River Somme.

OVERLEAF: British troops advance under cover of a smoke screen in Northern France.

square." But when the battalion was drafted overseas he was transferred to another and left behind. "It was a terrible blow to my pride," he recalled, "the worst in my life." He went to see Lord Kitchener, the all-powerful Secretary of State for War, who had so decreed his fate. "What does it matter if I am killed?" he insisted. "I have four brothers."

Lord Kitchener replied, with a steely look in his eyes: "If I were sure you would be killed, I do not know if I should be right to restrain you. But I cannot take the chance, which always exists until we have a settled line, of the enemy taking you prisoner." The Prince thus realized that, as he wryly expressed it, his trophy value exceeded his military usefulness.

Sure enough, as the German armies advanced swiftly on Paris and the British armies checked them at the Battle of the Marne, many of his friends and brother-officers died. His equerry, Major Cadogan, and two of his father's equerries were among the casualties, and he exclaimed in his diary: "I shan't have a friend left soon." At last, in November, after resolute pressure on those in au-

thority, he was sent to France as an officer on the staff of the Commander-in-Chief, Sir John French. He had enlisted the sympathy of an old friend of his grandfather, Sir Dighton Probyn, who wrote: "He came to wish me good-bye—and it really was delightful to see the change that had come over him since he had last been in this room. On the last occasion he really *cried* with sorrow at the idea of 'being disgraced' . . . Yesterday his face beamed with joy."

Disillusionment, however, was swift. G.H.Q., where he sat in an office doing paperwork, was thirty miles behind the front line, and, though he sometimes carried dispatches, his father had given instructions that he must not be sent into the forward areas. He felt himself "in a glass case." "Oh, not to be a Prince!" was the constant refrain of his thoughts. No "brass-hat" by nature, he yearned to be part of the rank and file. "My generation," as he afterwards wrote, "had a rendezvous with history, and my whole being insisted that I share the common destiny, whatever it might be."

Eventually however he was permitted to serve nearer to the front line, on the staff of the Guards Division. Here at last he was among friends. Though he was never permitted to fight, he saw fighting. Surveying the dead around him, with his Divisional Commander, after the abortive Battle of Loos, he "got some idea of the horror and ghastliness of it all. . . . Those dead bodies offered a most pathetic and gruesome sight. Too cruel to be killed within a few yds. of yr. objective after a 300 yds. sprint of death!! This was my 1st real sight of war, & it moved and impressed me most enormously!!" On returning to his car he found it riddled with bullet-holes, and his driver killed by a burst of shrapnel.

This narrow escape made his superior officers the more anxious for his safety. "The risks," one of them reported home, "will be accentuated by H.R.H.'s enthusiasm." Like a truant schoolboy, he was forever eluding their vigilance. One night he borrowed a dispatch-rider's motor-cycle, and started out towards the trenches. But he ran it into a shell-hole which was invisible in the darkness; the motor-bike was wrecked and he was found some hours later by a search party, covered in mud and playing cards in a dug-out, by the light of a candle, with a group of French *poilus*. He became known to his staff as "Dynamite Wales," from his habit of going off at any moment, and a general wrote, when the Prince was transferred from his command, "Thank Heaven he's going. This job will turn my hair grey. He insists on tramping in the front lines."

As time went on the policing of his movement near the front was relaxed. He had other escapes as narrow as the first, and saw more of the grim and sordid side of modern warfare. And the fighting men saw the Prince, gaining courage from his proximity as a companion in arms. They wrote of him in their letters

OPPOSITE: The Prince of Wales in France, where he spent his first six months as A.D.C. to the Commander-in-Chief, Sir John French. OVERLEAF: Kaiser Wilhelm II of Germany frequently toured the battlefronts. Standing behind him is his son Prinz Wilhelm, who was removed from the Death's Head Hussars, and then led the Fifth Army in 1914.

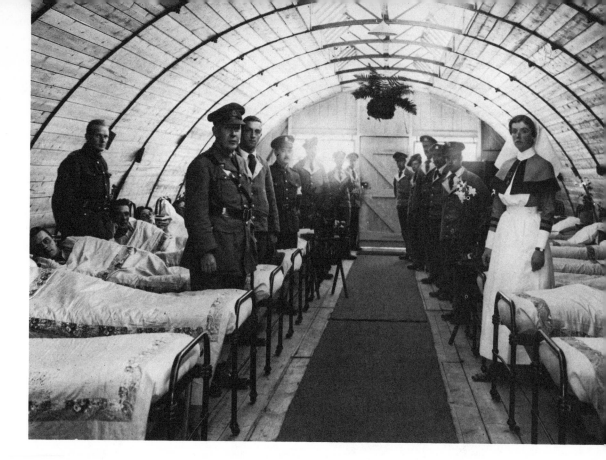

Queen Mary visited France and inspected military hospital wards, such as this one in a Nissen hut.

home: "He is among the keenest and hardest soldiers"; he was "in a house which was rocking and shaking all night under the constant detonation of bombardment"; "I never saw anyone look so well as the Prince of Wales. He is simply full of vim and has a real weather-beaten look, and is as wiry as a cat." "The Prince is always in the thick of it," wrote a private in the Coldstream Guards. "Only last night he passed me when the German shells were coming over. . . . I hope, please God, he will come home safe and sound without a scratch." His brother-officers in the Welsh Guards would say, "A bad shelling will always produce the Prince of Wales or Llewellyn Jones!"—a raw-boned Welsh chaplain with whom he made friends after giving him a lift on the road near Armentières.

More formally, the Commander-in-Chief wrote in a dispatch of his satisfactory progress. "I have myself been very favourably impressed by the quickness with which His Royal Highness has acquired knowledge of the various branches of the service and the deep interest he has always displayed in the comfort and welfare of the men. His visits to the troops, both in the field and in hospitals, have been greatly appreciated by all ranks. His Royal Highness did duty for a time in the trenches, with the Battalion to which he belongs." On these visits to hospitals he insisted on seeing the worst cases. Once, visiting a man disfigured beyond recognition, he leaned over the bed and touched his cheek with his lips. The part played by the Prince of Wales in the war was hardly as "insignificant" as he would afterwards modestly insist.

In the spring of 1916 he was transferred for a spell to Egypt, where he inspected and helped to prepare a report on the defences of the Suez Canal. He inspected also some of the country's ancient monuments. But, as he was a creature of his age, the chief pleasure he took in the Pyramids lay in hitting a golf ball from the summit of one of them.

The most significant fruits of this trip to the Middle Eastern front were his encounters with the Dominion troops, the Australians and New Zealanders— the "Anzacs"—evacuated from Gallipoli, whom for the first time he came to know and understand and appreciate. With his directness and simplicity he made an immediate appeal to their affections, giving personal substance to their sense of affinity with Britain and loyalty to the Crown. Back in France, he made a point of mixing, whenever he could, with these soldiers of the Empire, heightening morale as he walked among them and talked to them in the free-and-easy manner of any colonial officer.

The Prince inspects a workshop where women have taken over men's jobs.

Years later a South African general remarked to an English friend, "I don't think people have any idea what an asset that boy was over there!" The war indeed turned the Prince into the perfect "mixer," and as such a major potential asset to his country. After it, he was able to say, with complete justification, "In those four years I mixed with men. In those four years I found my manhood."

The Prince of Wales celebrated his twenty-first birthday in France. But a message was issued from Buckingham Palace requesting in his name that all congratulations, public or otherwise, should be postponed until the conclusion of the war. In February 1918, recalled home to make the first of many tours of the industrial areas, he took his seat in the House of Lords. A few months later he made his first official visit abroad, as an ambassador for his country, to help boost Italian morale with a message from his father and an assurance of British friendship towards Italy. He was treated to a public ovation all the more rapturous because of the fact that, in the meantime, he had served for a spell as a staff officer

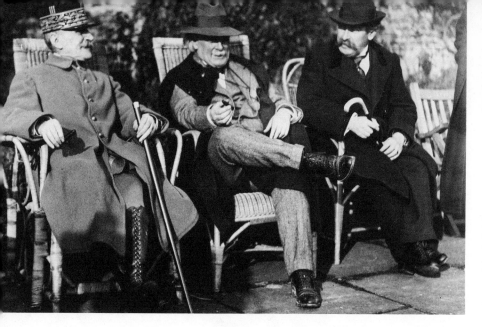

OPPOSITE: The Prince in Normandy. ABOVE: After the war, David Lloyd George chats with Marshal Foch and the French Prime Minister, Aristide Briand, in the garden of Chequers, country home of the Prime Minister. RIGHT: President Woodrow Wilson, who recommended a declaration to Congress in 1917 that a state of war existed between the United States and Germany. In November 1918 he was present at the signing of the Peace Treaty at Versailles, with Lloyd George and Clemenceau.

OVERLEAF: Piccadilly Circus. Crowds stand to attention in observance of three minutes' silence on Armistice Day.

on the Italian front, helping to halt the retreat from Caporetto. It was a visit that gave rise to hopes, translated into baseless rumours, that he would marry the daughter of the King of Italy, Princess Yolanda.

The end of the war found him back in France, on the staff of the Canadian Corps. From its headquarters, as central Europe crumbled, he wrote to his father: "There seems to be a regular epidemic of revolutions and abdications throughout the enemy countries, which certainly makes it a hard and critical time for the remaining monarchies; but of those that remain, I have no hesitation in saying that ours is by far the [most] solid tho. of course it must be kept so & I more than realise that this can only be done by keeping in the closest possible touch with the people & I can promise you that this point is always at the back of my mind & that I am & always shall make every effort to carry out, as I know how vitally it will influence the future of the Empire!!"

Small wonder that, on the night of the peace celebrations, the London crowds were not content with the appearance, on the balcony of Buckingham Palace, of the King and Queen. This time they shouted too for the Prince of Wales. For he had caught their imagination, as a symbol of the new generation. He came out onto the balcony amid enthusiastic cheers from the people. Already he was being cast for his post-war role of Prince Charming.

Chapter IV

*T*he world into which the Prince of Wales had grown up was a new world, heralding a new way of life. The more rigid conventions of past generations were to be swept away. Youth was to be free, to live as it chose, by its own standards. The people were to be free, to live by the standards of a true popular democracy. There were to be "homes fit for heroes to live in." The Prince of Wales, twenty-five years old, now emerged on to the stage as the living embodiment of the hopes of British youth and the British people—of people of all classes, from all parts of the Empire.

It was the Celtic imagination of the victorious Prime Minister, Lloyd George, with his sense of people and his sense of "theatre," that first saw the potentialities of the Prince as a popular hero. He was young, he was attractive, he was unassuming, he was eager for life. During the war, serving his country, he had acquired the happy faculty of mixing with men of all sorts and classes. He had, above all things, a natural charm.

It was Lloyd George's concern to hold the Empire together, to weld those bonds with its various peoples which had been forged as they fought side by side in the war, to forestall any weakening of allegiance to the Crown which their various post-war upheavals might bring. He saw that this could best be achieved by personal contact, and that the person to achieve it was the heir to the Crown himself. He thus evolved the idea of sending the Prince on a series of tours to the Dominions to thank them, on his father's behalf, for their contributions to the war. To the Prince himself he explained that his own personal appearance in far corners of the Empire could do more to calm any discord than half a dozen solemn imperial conferences. King George V at once agreed.

In the uniform of the Scots Fusiliers.

The officers and crew of the United States Navy Curtiss flying-boat NC-4, who made a transatlantic flight via the Azores and Portugal the month before Alcock and Brown's non-stop flight, were entertained at the House of Commons in 1919. OPPOSITE: The Prince of Wales chatting with Winston Churchill, Secretary of State for War and Air. ABOVE: The Prince with the American airmen on the terrace of the House. In the group are Lord Reading, in tails, and Commander Albert Read of the NC-4, whose face partially obscures Admiral Wemyss, First Sea Lord.

H.M.S. *Renown* departs for Canada.

The Prince of Wales thus left for Canada in the summer of 1919 in H.M.S. *Renown,* the British battle-cruiser which was to be his floating home during the next few years. A retinue of twenty accompanied him. His father, who had himself made a stately progress through the dominion in his own youth, gave him a number of parting injunctions. "You have had a much freer life than I ever knew," he said. "The war has made it possible for you to mix with all manner of people in a way I was never able to do. But don't think this means that you can act like other people. You must always remember your position and who you are." His father's Keeper of the Privy Purse, Sir Frederick Ponsonby, was more specific: "If I may say so, Sir," he said, "I think there is a risk in your making yourself too accessible. . . . A prince should not show himself too much. The monarchy must remain on a pedestal. . . . If you bring it down to the people it will lose its mystery and influence."

The Prince of Wal‍‍‍‍‍‍‍‍‍‍‍‍‍‍‍‍‍‍‍‍‍‍nd said so. He realized that an age of social change had dawn‍‍‍‍‍‍‍‍‍tic preparation for life had shown him that he himself was mu‍‍‍‍‍‍‍‍‍ple, and he was convinced that the monarchy, for which he s‍‍‍‍‍‍‍‍‍ step down from its pedestal and move closer to the ordinar‍‍‍‍‍‍‍‍‍he saw it, was to give this mysterious and aloof institution a ‍‍‍‍‍‍‍‍‍These ideas of his were now to be put to the test at the sta‍‍‍‍‍‍‍‍‍h mass communications were becoming a paramount influe‍‍‍ce. Radio was ‍‍‍‍‍‍‍‍loping, so were photography, the news film, the popular press. The Prince of Wales became, as it were, the first "star" of these new public media, through which millions of people, all over the world, watched his progress around it.

The Prince first stepped into the New World at St. John's in Newfoundland, where he passed through a triumphal arch "largely composed of drums of cod-liver oil, and hung with the carcases of dried cod-fish." In his first speech he said: "This is a red-letter day for me, as I have just set foot for the first time on Canadian soil. . . . I do not feel that I have come to this great Dominion as a stranger, since I have been so closely associated with the Dominion troops during the war, and made so many friends among them. . . . I want Canada to look upon me as a Canadian, if not actually by birth, certainly in mind and spirit!" He was to look back on these first days as the most exhilarating in all his experience.

Arriving at Quebec he was swept into crowds of tens of thousands, "so volatile and vigorous as to constitute at times an almost terrifying phenomenon." As the people pressed around him, cheering and yelling and snatching at his handkerchief and tugging at the buttons on his coat, he became anxious less for his own safety than for that of his well-wishers themselves. The State processions were on horseback, in the traditional style of the past, and he became especially concerned lest the horses, untrained to such ceremonial, should take fright and trample the crowds underfoot. And sure enough, at a parade of twenty-seven thousand ex-servicemen who broke their ranks and swarmed around him, the Prince had to be lifted from the back of his quivering steed and passed by strong hands over the heads of the crowd, to be deposited on the platform. Thenceforward there were no more equestrian functions.

The Prince progressed in a royal train across most of the continent. At every stop he made extempore three-minute speeches from his observation platform, learning to think on his feet as he spoke. He would step down from the train, not onto a red carpet but onto the line, informally mixing and talking and exchanging war reminiscences with farm-hands, miners, workingmen, as no prince touring his dominions had ever done before. He was proved immediately right in his conviction that mere civility—the polite but distant bow, the right word to the right person, a mild interest in a carefully selected assortment of

The ranch near Calgary, bought by the Prince when his imagination was fired by the life of the Rocky Mountain foothills.

local projects and good works—was no longer an adequate royal "export," as it had been in his father's time.

In the towns invitations to his receptions were extended not to a select few but to the whole population. In Toronto he received half a million guests. Everywhere they would queue for hours for the privilege of a handshake. "Put it right here, Ed," demanded a veteran, "I shook hands with your grandfather." He shook so many hands that his right hand gave out, becoming dangerously swollen, and the left had to be called into service.

In Ottawa he adroitly appeared at the head of a Labour Day procession to open the new Parliament building. In a mining region, near Winnipeg, a new vein of silver was named after him, and he was given a town "to do what he liked with." In the Rockies he was invested with a huge feather head-dress as chief of an Indian tribe, with the title of Chief Morning Star. At a parade in Toronto, before forty thousand spectators, he caused transports of enthusiasm by sprinting after a wounded soldier's hat, blown off by the wind, and replacing it firmly on his head. He won the hearts of the West by mounting a bronco and leading a cowboy charge. He won them more permanently by buying, on an impulse, a cattle ranch in Alberta, a "home from home" so that his farewell to Canada would be only *au revoir*.

Lloyd George had shrewdly judged that what the Dominions wanted was "a first-class carnival in which the Prince of Wales should play a gay, many-sided and natural role." They got it—and more. Underlying it, the Prince's task, as he saw it, was to demonstrate to the Dominions the vitality of the Mother Country and the spirit of democracy. He did so by demonstrating his own vitality and his own accessibility. The Canadians revered him because he was the heir to the Throne. But at the same time they loved him because, throughout all his public appearances, he remained his personal self. Beneath the dignity of the heir apparent they found themselves charmed by the spontaneity, the friendliness, the adaptability, the zest of a lively young man. The image he left with them was an image of youth, which promised well for the new age in Britain. Through it they began to see the Mother Country no longer as a proud, aloof, conservative power but as a flexible, go-ahead democratic civilization, with a royal family which was close to the people and had their interests at heart.

On the Prince's return Lloyd George described his tour as not merely a triumph but an opportune triumph. "The Throne," he declaimed in a speech, "means a great deal in this country. It means even more to the Empire. Throughout all climes, through all continents, there is no institution—Parliament, laws, ecclesiastical organizations, not even language—of which it can be said that it is common to the whole Empire. But the Throne unites them all. You have to read what happened in Canada to see that the Empire is stronger today for that tour. . . . The welcome was not an organized one; it welled from the hearts of a brave people, and you can see it in every line that comes from Canada and in every word you hear of what happened there. The Prince of Wales struck the right note. He greeted Canada as a nation, as a nation that had won the spurs of nationhood in the great conflict of the nations for freedom and for civilization. And that was part of his success."

Meanwhile from Canada the Prince, at his own desire, had crossed the border into Maine for a ten-day trip to America. This was the first visit of a Prince of Wales to the United States since that of his grandfather, half a century earlier. After observing the two minutes' silence, on the first anniversary of the Armistice, in his train in Baltimore station, he received an enthusiastic reception in Washington. President Wilson was ill, but he saw him for a few moments in bed—Lincoln's bed—in the White House and reflected that "his was the most disappointed face that I had ever looked upon. If this was the condition in which the cares of high office left a man, then as a Prince I was happy to be spared the ravages of party politics." He won the hearts of the hard-bitten journalists by a speech at the National Press Club in which he modestly disclaimed a knowledge of public affairs to equal theirs, and added, "Your institutions, your ways of life, your aims are as democratic as ours, and the atmosphere in which I find myself is the same invigorating and familiar atmosphere I have always noted in American friends."

In November 1919. OPPOSITE: On the steps of the White House after visiting President Wilson, who was ill in bed. ABOVE: Out walking with Theodore Roosevelt, Jr., before the Prince left Washington for New York City.

New York gave him an ear-splitting harbour welcome, and a "snowstorm" of ticker-tape showered down upon him as he drove up Broadway to be presented by the Mayor with "the freedom of this greatest city of the wonder republic of the ages." He mounted to the top of the Woolworth Building, visited Grant's Tomb, the Stock Exchange, the Metropolitan Opera, and the *Ziegfeld Follies,* attended a magnificent ball given in his honour by Mrs. Whitelaw Reid in her Madison Avenue house, was received at West Point by its superintendent, a young brigadier-general named Douglas MacArthur, laid a wreath on the grave of Theodore Roosevelt at Oyster Bay, and planted a tree, as his grandfather had done, in Central Park.

Everywhere his welcome was rapturous. "They Princed me so much," he joked afterwards, "that I had the greatest difficulty in refraining from barking!" But in this country where royalty inspired curiosity rather than reverence, it was a "Princing" that saw through the Prince to the man. "It was not entirely because he was Prince of Wales," an American wrote, "but more particularly because we liked him." As the New York *Sun* summed it up: "It's the smile of him, the natural, fun-loving spirit that twinkles in his blue eyes." There was hopeful speculation in the press and elsewhere that he had come to seek an American bride. This was not his intention. Nevertheless, among all his American recollections, there lingered on his mind the words and music of a song he had heard at the *Ziegfeld Follies*: "A Pretty Girl Is Like a Melody."

In New York City. OPPOSITE: Reviewing American sailors at the Battery.
ABOVE: Crowds in Wall Street give the Prince a rousing welcome before he
tours Manhattan.

OVERLEAF: Sightseeing, and receiving a wreath from two girls, to be placed
on the statue of Joan of Arc.

95

A scene from the *Ziegfeld Follies,* 1919. The Prince particularly enjoyed the hit song, "A Pretty Girl Is Like a Melody." OPPOSITE: The Metropolitan Opera programme and Enrico Caruso as Canio in *I Pagliacci,* the role he sang at the special performance for the Prince, November 18.

98

This Theatre when filled to its capacity, can be emptied in five minutes. Choose the nearest exit now and in case of need walk quietly (do not run) to that exit in order to avoid panic

METROPOLITAN OPERA HOVSE

SPECIAL PERFORMANCE
IN HONOR OF
HIS ROYAL HIGHNESS THE PRINCE OF WALES

Tuesday Evening, November 18th at 9 o'clock

PROGRAMME

1. OBERON .... *Weber*
OVERTURE
Scene 3, Act 1: Hall in the Harem of the Caliph

REZIA .... FLORENCE EASTON
FATIMA .... KATHLEEN HOWARD

Conductor—ARTUR BODANZKY

2. SAMSON ET DALILA .... *Saint-Saens*
Ballet and Chorus from Scene 2, Act 3: Interior of Temple of Dagon
Incidental Dance by LILYAN OGDEN, and the Corps de Ballet

Conductor—GIUSEPPE BAMBOSCHEK

3. PAGLIACCI .... *Leoncavallo*
Act 1. Outskirts of a Village in Calabria

NEDDA .... FLORENCE EASTON
CANIO .... ENRICO CARUSO
TONIO .... PASQUALE AMATO
BEPPE .... GIORDANO PALTRINIERI
SILVIO .... MARIO LAURENTI

Conductor—ROBERTO MORANZONI

PROGRAMME CONTINUED ON NEXT PAGE   HARDMAN PIANO USED EXCLUSIVELY

Reviewing cadets at West Point Military Academy with Brigadier General Douglas MacArthur, Superintendent.

After less than four months at home, the Prince was off on his travels once more—this time to New Zealand and Australia. The message he was carrying to the Dominions had crystallized: "I come to you as the King's eldest son, as heir to a Throne that stands for a heritage of common aims and ideals—that provides the connecting link of a Commonwealth whose members are free to develop, each on his own lines, but all to work together as one."

After touching at Barbados, where the Prince scotched rumours of a political deal with America by asserting, "The King's subjects are not for sale," the *Renown* passed through the Panama Canal. In Panama, at a dance in his honour, he chose as partner an attractive girl of whom the local pundits did not wholly approve. It was explained to him tactfully that she was an assistant in a drug store. "Well," he replied, "it must be a jolly good drug store." He danced with her again, then did his duty with other ladies of more appropriate social standing.

After visits to San Diego and Hawaii, the ship moved southwards and the Prince, for the first time, "crossed the line," thus entering the traditional domain of "King Neptune." Invested with the "Companionship of the Order of the Equatorial Bath," he replied with the verse—

> "I know I'm for it, King—so, boys,
> Don't let me keep the party waiting."

He then submitted, before the hirsute ruler and his court, to the customary ritual prescribed for such newcomers:

> Shave him and bash him,
> Duck him and splash him,
> Torture and smash him
> And don't let him go.

Thus the *Renown* sailed into the harbour of Auckland, capital of "the last, loneliest, and loveliest" of the Dominions—New Zealand. The New Zealanders gave him a warm but decorous welcome, and as he travelled through their country he was continually reminded of his own. Even a railway strike did not ruffle his programme, since the strikers, respecting his non-party status, allowed the royal train to run. Only the Maoris, the indigenous inhabitants of the islands, struck an exotic and unfamiliar note as they sang and danced before him in their picturesque head-dresses and costumes. Queen Victoria was still a living legend to them, and they were as excited as children to hear the words of her great-grandson: "I will ever keep before me the pattern of Victoria, the great Queen, whose heart was with the Maori people from the day on which they swore allegiance to their ruler."

Australia was a more arduous assignment. Imperial preferences, Lloyd George had warned the Prince, are not all the same. The Australians, as he already knew from his wartime contacts, were a tough people, independently minded and quick to resent interference. They had no undue respect for the trappings of royalty and were at this time in the throes of a political conflict between their National Government and a vociferous Labour Opposition. "The Australians," the Governor-General warned him, "must be handled with care. They hate formality."

As the Prince of Wales drove through a crowd of three-quarters of a million people, lining the Melbourne streets, there were ribald cries of "Oh, Percy, where did you get that hat?" But the crowd was essentially friendly and gay, and reserved its boos for the rival politicians, Mr. Hughes the Prime Minister and Mr. Storey the Opposition leader, whom his enemies described as "red all through." The Prince lost no time in winning the friendship of both, and was soon the hero of the Australian people. They called him "Digger" like one of themselves. There was a mass impulse to touch him, to prod some part of the Prince of Wales. And the prods were slaps and blows so vigorous that he was often black-and-blue with bruises.

"The people of Australia," the Prime Minister declared to the Prince in his speech of welcome, "see in you the things which they believe." The Sydney

At Perth, on his visit to Australia.

An informal portrait in Honolulu, on his way back from Australia.

Sun, an independent newspaper, wrote of him more personally: "Before the Prince landed the popular idea of princes was of something haughty and remote, but this smiling, appealing, youthful man . . . smiled away the difference which Australians believed lay between royalty and the commonalty."

In Sydney, a Socialist stronghold, where he diplomatically wore a jacket and soft brown hat in place of his naval uniform, the Prince's welcome was even more tumultuous. He travelled upcountry and in a mere two months visited some hundred towns, in all the states of the Dominion. He came to love "its bigness, its adventurousness, its courage." He displayed a light-hearted courage himself when his train was derailed among the lumber camps of Western Australia. By the time he reached Tasmania he had made so many speeches that his voice was reduced to a whisper.

When he left Australia, "half-killed by kindness," he was "physically and mentally at the end of [his] tether!" But he had, in the words of an Australian journalist quoted by the London *Times*, "silenced criticism of the Monarchy for current lifetimes." He returned with a new mature knowledge of himself and a truer understanding of the Empire and its problems, which he did his best, from now onwards, to communicate to the people, and to those in authority, at home.

102

Chapter V

At last the Prince of Wales was to have a year at home—but no more. The most formidable of all his youthful tasks now awaited him—an official tour of the great subcontinent of India, the "brightest jewel" in his father's imperial crown. Here was a situation distinctly more explosive than the domestic disputes of Australia. For India was already in the throes of that political unrest which was to lead, after another world war, to its secession from the Empire.

King George V, who had twice made a stately progress through India, instructed his son as to how he should act there. "You seem," he said, "to have evolved a new technique of your own in the carrying out of your Commonwealth missions, and, while I do not altogether approve your informal approach, I must concede that you have done very well. But you must not forget that India is entirely different from Canada, New Zealand, and Australia. What went down well with the white people in those three dominions will not go down at all in India." He gave him a severe and emphatic injunction: "You are to do exactly as *they* tell you. *They* know best." By "they" he meant the British civil and military authorities, those *"pukka sahibs"* who were the Anglo-Indian ruling caste.

One of them, a retired Indian civil servant named Sir Walter Lawrence, who had acted as his father's Chief of Staff in India, chanced in that summer of 1921 to be staying at Balmoral, where the Prince was building up his strength in the bracing air of the moors for the arduous task that confronted him in the months to come. Sir Walter briefed him at length as to the nature of India, with its complex political and social systems, and expressed to him his own conservative hopes for its future, as a dominion ruled by its princes with British advice. But he made one practical suggestion—that the Prince should learn enough Urdu, the predominant Indian language, to enable him to make simple speeches

The Prince of Wales in naval uniform at the age of twenty-seven.

An enthusiastic welcome at Aden, on his way to India.

With his cousin Lord Louis Mountbatten (nearest the camera), on a pig-sticking expedition in India.

and talk in their own tongue with as many Indians as possible. "I wish," he added regretfully, "I had had the foresight to suggest the same thing to His Majesty your father years ago." The Prince eagerly took his advice, which seemed to offer him the prospect of a closer approach to the Indian crowd. The "good mixer" in the heir to the Throne died hard.

Passing through the Red Sea after a visit to Malta, the *Renown* touched at Aden, where a banner enjoined him to TELL DADDY WE ARE ALL HAPPY UNDER BRITISH RULE. All the inhabitants of India were not so happy. The Mahatma Gandhi, leader of the radical Congress Party and a dedicated enemy of the British Raj, had lately launched his campaign of "non-co-operation" with the Government of India, carrying with him a large section of the educated classes who lived in the towns. In Bombay, where the *Renown* docked, he had called upon his disciples to stage a strike on the day of the Prince's arrival, and to drape their houses in black as a sign of mourning for British rule. The Prince was thus faced with the prospect of "empty streets, insulting placards, and perhaps even incidents of violence."

Landing on a red carpet, with traditional ceremony, he proceeded with the Viceroy, Lord Reading, to a gilded pavilion, emblazoned with the royal coat-of-arms. Here he delivered, to an assembly of be-medalled, gold-braided officials and ruling princes decked in jewels and shimmering silks, a message of greeting from his father, the King-Emperor. To this he added a more personal phrase of his own: "I want to know you and I want you to know me." Then, arrayed in full-dress naval uniform of tropical white, with a sun-helmet on his head and a gold-embroidered umbrella held over it, the Prince drove in processional State, in a horse-drawn carriage, to Government House.

Despite Gandhi's boycott, thousands of Indians lined the streets, and there came from them, as he afterwards recalled, "a sound such as I have never elsewhere heard issue from human lips—not so much a cheer as an immense murmur of delight, punctuated by the rippling sounds of the hand-clapping that is the Oriental customary sign of approval." Though Gandhi had failed to spoil the show, there were outbreaks during the next few days of organized hooliganism, with communal street-fights and firing by police to restore order. But these riots interrupted the official programme on one occasion only, when a visit to a school was cancelled for the sake of the children's safety.

This was the first of a series of displays of imperial pageantry, to be re-enacted over the length and breadth of India with a pomp and splendour dear to the heart of the Orient. As its hero the Prince played his role with all the solemnity and dignity required of an heir to the Throne, sustaining in public functions a formal demeanour which impressed the Indians as his freer and easier manner had charmed the Australians. He did his best to mix with them.

But for security reasons he was seldom allowed to drive through their bazaars and native quarters. As a rule, they saw the Prince only in procession through the European quarters, held back by cordons of police which he himself often criticized as excessive. Nevertheless, beneath the mask and the mystique of majesty, they sensed his good fellowship, the private self not wholly submerged by the public.

Meanwhile Gandhi, in his well-organized campaign for a boycott, was putting pressure on the people by intimidation in various forms. He was partially successful. But so was the Prince. In Lucknow the students refused to join in the university sports, the Indian shops were shut, and the cab-drivers went on strike, so that loyal Indians could not travel into the city from the country outside. But the British Army put lorries on the streets, bearing notices in Urdu: COME AND SEE THE PRINCE AND HAVE A FREE RIDE, and Indians soon crowded into them.

In the holy city of Benares the Prince's reception was mixed, but the university students acclaimed him, and he won admiration by conversing in Urdu. In Calcutta, though the English-language press described his entry as a "triumph without a discordant note," the Indian press played it down, insisting that his reception fell far short of the standard set on previous royal visits. Thousands remained in their houses in obedience to Gandhi, and the cries in the streets were mixed. But later—as in other cities where he spent any length of time—curiosity prevailed, the crowds at the various functions became increasingly Indian, and, in the words of an official report, "the enthusiasm towards His Royal Highness continued to grow."

In Agra the doors of the closed shops bore the sign, NO WELCOME TO THE PRINCE. But he entered Delhi, the Imperial capital, "amidst a hurricane of cheers," and his visit to a camp of twenty-five thousand "Untouchables" prompted the Chief Commissioner's verdict: "I am informed by non-official workers among these depressed classes that this recognition has had a most remarkable effect in stimulating their self-respect and in strengthening their determination to lift themselves out of the thraldom which custom and caste regulations have hitherto assigned to their lot."

In Lahore trouble was expected. But anxious officials "stared with amazement" as, at a big native gathering, the Prince rode slowly among thousands of Punjabis, dressed not in official uniform but in ordinary riding clothes. They marvelled at his unroyal simplicity, and when he left in the evening the station platform was "a seething mass of excited and gesticulating humanity." At Peshawar, on the north-west frontier, Gandhi's policy rebounded against him, as the police, detailed to protect the Prince, found themselves protecting the followers of the Mahatma instead, against attacks by loyal tribesmen.

Arrival at the Gates of Victoria, Calcutta, 1922.

Gandhi's greatest success was in Allahabad, the city of Pandit Nehru, whom the authorities had imprisoned on the eve of the Prince's arrival. Here he found himself driving in an ominous silence between shuttered houses, through streets deserted but for the troops which lined the route. It was, as he put it, "a spooky experience." Only at the corners of side-streets did he see Indians peering furtively out for a view of the procession. But when, later in the day, he played polo in a match between his staff and a regimental team, taking his pick from among the twenty-five polo ponies which he carried on his train, the Indians, a nation of sportsmen, turned out in their thousands to watch and applaud him. Loyalty to Nehru could not control them indefinitely. "The natives," explained the Governor, "will do as they like from now on." In the morning his bearing as a prince might have won their homage; in the evening his prowess as a horseman won their hearts.

Mahatma Gandhi.

In surmounting these various hazards, the Prince showed ample courage and resource. In himself he had moods of discouragement. Once he wrote to his father: "I'm very depressed about my work in British India as I don't feel that I'm doing a scrap of good—in fact I can say that I know I am not."

But in the native states, semi-feudal principalities loyal to Britain and free from the influence of Gandhi, he could feel more at home and relax. Here he relished Oriental hospitality on a sumptuous scale, and particularly sport of all kinds. He learned pig-sticking in Jodhpur, and later won a hog-hunters' horse-race. In Mysore he played squash rackets with the Maharaja and saw wild elephants trapped and trained. He rode home on an elephant after an entertainment by the devil-dancers of Kashmir. He shot sand-grouse at Bikanir and inspected its Camel Corps, whose camels he had ridden in Egypt. He shot tigers in Nepal, where for six weeks ten thousand Nepalese had laboured to build miles of roads and clear the site for his camp. In Baroda, where the people and their ruler, the Gaekwar, gilded themselves and their elephants in his honour, he hunted black buck with cheetahs.

In Gwalior he was greeted by the Maharaja's two children, dressed in khaki uniforms and named respectively George and Mary, after his parents. In Hyderabad the subjects of the Nizam, with his fabulous wealth, held their babies before him in the air so that they should grow up with the blessing of having seen the Prince of Wales. In Indore he hung garlands around the necks of eighteen princes. In Udaipur, with its fabulous water palaces, the Maharana, a descendant of the Sun, encouraged him: "I am sure Your Royal Highness's popularity will exercise a soothing and healing effect on the present situation in India."

The Prince paid a week's visit to Burma, where the political situation was calmer, and where his opportune presence lost ground for the nationalist movement. When he finally left India, too exhausted yet to appreciate the full fruits of his visit, a newspaper wrote that he "had done more to establish the relations between the masses of India and the Crown on a solid basis of personal contact in four months than edicts could have done in a generation." From Karachi the *Renown* proceeded via Ceylon, Malaya, and Hong Kong to Japan, where the Prince was the official guest, for a month, of the Prince Regent, Hirohito, and was able to travel more freely.

After eight months of travel he landed once more in England, in June 1922. At a banquet in his honour at the Guildhall in London, Lloyd George proposed his health in the following words of praise:

> "Whatever our feeling for him was before he went to India, it is deeper today. It was a high act of statesmanship, carried through with inimitable gifts of grace, of tact, and of a drawing attachment which is so very much his dominant characteristic. More than that, it was a high act of courage carried through with faultless nerve. There were many who doubted the wisdom of the visit. There was no one who was not anxious about the visit. There were difficulties, there were menaces, there was an atmosphere which gave great concern to everyone. He went there without fear. He went indomitably at the call of duty, and whatever the Empire owed to him before, it owes him a debt which it can never repay today."

ABOVE: The royal barge, with the Prince of Wales on board, tours a lake in Rangoon.

In Japan in 1922. ABOVE: "Duck-netting" in the grounds of the Hama Palace, Tokyo. LEFT: Shooting the rapids and waving a Japanese flag, on the Hosugawa River at Kyoto. BELOW: Feeding the tame deer in the garden of the public hall at Nara.

BELOW: After his world tour, the Prince drives in procession with his father, the Duke of York, and Prince Henry. RIGHT: Waving to the crowds that had gathered to greet him in front of Buckingham Palace.

Chapter VI

*O*n St. George's Day, 1923, the Prince
of Wales, in his role as Ambassador and protagonist of Empire, presided over a
great British Empire exhibition at Wembley, designed to display the industrial
and other products of Britain's overseas territories. It drew visitors to Britain
not only from the Dominions but from all parts of the world. In a speech of
welcome to his father, who opened it, the Prince described the exhibition as a
"living history of the Empire and its present structure." It would, he was sure,
show the world that the most powerful agency of civilization had its heart set
upon peaceful aims and the good of mankind. It should impress the peoples of
the Empire itself with a sense of their responsibilities, teaching them not to be
"slothful stewards" but to work unitedly and energetically to develop their
resources for the benefit of the British race, and its own various races, and for
the benefit of mankind in general.

April 1923. Lady Elizabeth Bowes-Lyon leaves No. 17 Bruton Street for Westminster Abbey.
OPPOSITE: After the wedding ceremony, the Duke of York with his bride at Buckingham Palace.

116

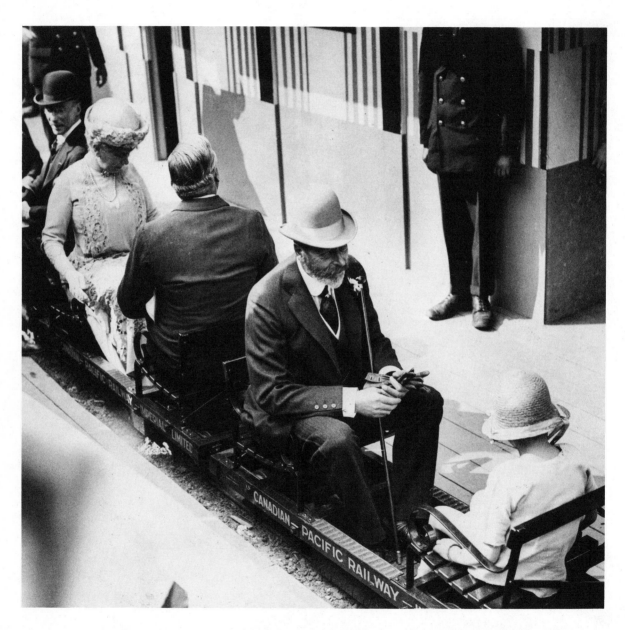

The King and Queen take a ride on the model railway at the British Empire Exhibition at Wembley in 1924. OPPOSITE: The Prince of Wales enjoying the roller-coaster with the Duke and Duchess of York in the amusement grounds.

OVERLEAF: The Prince of Wales and Admiral of the Fleet, Lord Beatty, dine at the Royal Naval Volunteer Reserve Club in London. The attendants are dressed in the uniform worn by sailors in the days of Horatio Nelson at the end of the eighteenth century.

H.M.S. *Repulse* leaving Portsmouth.

In the spring of 1925 he set off on the fourth and last of his official Empire tours, to the continent of Africa, thus completing Lloyd George's design for a Princely Odyssey to all the world's British communities. This time he sailed in the *Repulse,* sister-ship of the *Renown,* which had gone into dock.

First he visited the colonies of West Africa, the first Prince of Wales to set foot in this tropical region which was traditionally known as "the White Man's Grave." Much had changed since the Empire-builders of Sierre Leone greeted one another each morning with the query, "How many died last night?" For medical science had at last discovered that yellow fever arose not from the vapours but from the malarial mosquito, an insect now under control.

Native habits too had changed, as the Prince was to find in a series of "palavers" with African chiefs, since the days when Prempeh, the notorious King of the Ashanti, presided over orgies of human sacrifice and was reputed to paint the walls of his palace twice each year with human blood. In the year of the Prince's birth he had been exiled by the British authorities to an island in the Indian Ocean. But now he had returned, no longer a bloodthirsty tyrant but a respectable middle-aged gentleman, immaculately clothed in a black morning-jacket, striped trousers, white spats, white kid gloves, and a white sun-helmet, the only black face among the white officials assembled on the Royal Stand to receive the heir to the Imperial Throne. He was now plain Mr. Prempeh, a fervent convert to Christianity, who studied books on sanitation and confided to the Prince that he hoped soon to be elected Mayor of Kumasi. His magic word was now "progress, much progress," causing the Prince to reflect on the beneficence of British imperial rule. Here surely was the living embodiment of its justice, humanitarianism, and sagacity.

Before the Prince of Wales and Mr. Prempeh, whom the Ashantis still regarded as their overlord, was a mighty gathering of their chieftains, ranged beneath a hundred and fifty bright-coloured umbrellas of State, and adorned with crowns of glittering gold, while courtiers fanned them with elephants' tails. For this was the Gold Coast, and the town of Kumasi was built upon gold-dust. Paying homage, one after the other, to the son of the Great White King from beyond the seas, the chieftains presented him with a sword of pure native gold, cast by their goldsmiths with magic rites and then ceremoniously anointed with gin, the most costly and powerful liquid they knew. They presented him also with a model of the Golden Stool, the emblem of the sacred native monarchy for whose possession the British had fought in two Ashanti wars before bringing peace to the people. In an eloquent address to the Prince they swore allegiance and prayed, "May God, our Fetishes, and our Stools, guard and preserve you through your present Empire tour, restore you safely to your Royal Father, and give you long life and happiness."

On the road down to the coast at Accra, the Prince was welcomed in a series of ceremonies. The programme for his reception at Nsawam allowed for the presentation of various local representatives, namely:

> Old Christian Gentlemen
> Nobles and Richmen
> Respectable Merchants
> Respectable Ladies
> Two Aged People, and finally
> Two Youngsters.

His gifts were to be "a Gold casket, an antelope and an extraordinary size parrot." But the popular enthusiasm was such as to disrupt these proceedings. Bearing a large banner inscribed THE WESLEYANS OF NSAWAM GREET YOU, a half-naked crowd, beating tom-toms and shrieking with patriotic emotion, surged around the Prince so that it became impossible to make the presentations with proper solemnity. Thus the parrot escaped and the antelope, a miniature specimen, was lost in the crowd.

In Accra a Court poet presented the Prince with a manuscript ode in eight stanzas, of which here are three:

Hurrah for the Prince of Wales,
Glory for Ruler of waves.
Britannia's dearest Treasure
Appears on the Gold Coast shore.
God save the King & Prince,
Who so love the Province,
God save lovely Prince of Wales
Whose mighty ships rule the Waves.

Gold Coast's best lorries and cars,
Let them run from near and fars,
And soldiers march to and fro,
Governor and Prince shine through—
Nobles and Paramount Chiefs,
Let all come and none miss's
Yes, His Majesty's Son's hand
Will be shaken on this land.

He is the real Prince of Wales,
Born in the diamond Palace,
Dear Son of King George the Fifth
But he off the Palace leaves,
Wanders in dominions,
To know himself Nations,
Before getting the Gold Throne,
For which England hindrance thrown.

Less poetic, but no less appreciative, were the remarks on the Prince of other West African admirers:

"He open his face plenty. He talkum good. He be small boy but good feller. He be good past all men."

"I lookum proper. He catch young face, old eyes."

The highest praise was expressed by one exultant Negro: "He be small boy, he be young feller, but oh he be rascal!"

In Sierra Leone, West Africa, 1925. A garden party in Victoria Park, Freetown.

The Prince's last action on the Gold Coast was to dedicate the new building of the Achimota College, now a secondary school since the opening in 1948 of University College, the present university of the independent state of Ghana.

Next he visited Nigeria, travelling seven hundred miles upcountry to Kano, on the fringe of the Sahara Desert. Here he was treated to the greatest show of all, a magnificent Mounted Durbar, staged with tumultuous zest by twenty thousand tribal horsemen. It was a spectacle worthy of the martial glories of the Middle Ages, in which chieftains, some in chain-mail armour, others in tunics of leopard skin, many in brilliant flowing robes with turbans, rode on camels with finely wrought saddle-cloths or on horses caparisoned in harlequin quilts.

Court jesters capered on horseback among them. Slim mounted pages fanned their lords. Each tribe vied with the others in ferocious bearing and equestrian prowess as they galloped past the Prince or charged towards him, reining in sharply before his feet. Banners flared, lances glinted, scimitars flashed in salute. Above the pounding of a hundred thousand hooves shrill war-cries sounded; fanfares of horns and trumpets, often six feet long, and the skirl of an African bagpipe; the throbbing bass rhythms of a profusion of drums. As the Prince sat before the legions of warriors, young and slim in a State arm-chair, the horseman in him must often have itched to be riding among them.

In South Africa the Prince of Wales found, once more, an awkward political situation. His visit had been strongly encouraged by General Smuts, the great

General Smuts, who had encouraged the Prince's visit to South Africa, but who was no longer in power when he arrived there.

South African statesman and protagonist of closer relations with Britain. But his party had been defeated in the elections of the previous year, and the Nationalist Party of General Hertzog was now in power. It was composed of a hard core of Boer farmers, men of Dutch origin, who favoured ultimate secession from the Empire and the establishment of an independent South African republic. The Prince's arrival in Capetown thus coincided with a new phase in the hereditary feud between British and Dutch, which dated back to the British capture of the Dutch settlement of the Cape of Good Hope early in the nineteenth century, and led to two Boer Wars in the course of it. The Union of South Africa moreover was a polyglot dominion beset by other racial problems, and it was the Prince's invidious task to please not only the British and Dutch but the native Africans.

In Capetown, where he landed, he achieved an initial success at an all-party banquet given in his honour by the South African Parliament. Here, after his speech, he met with a demonstration of loyalty so unanimous that a senator remarked of it: "Nothing like this has ever occurred before in the history of this House." After dinner a Dutch Nationalist, who had fought against the British in the South African war and was known for his bitter anti-British feelings, went so far in his enthusiasm as to put an arm around the Prince's shoulder and announce in a voice for all to hear, "Prince, we want you to stop here with us and be our first President."

On the previous day he had been swept into a high-spirited "rag" by the students of Capetown University, a bilingual establishment where, according to the educational policy of the Union, both English and Dutch learned the African language of Afrikaans, and where lately the personality of the Prince of Wales had been put forward as a "voluntary subject" of study. Deciding to put it to the test when the Prince was due to attend a University function, a cavalcade of students, dressed as Boers and Zulus and notable figures of South African history, escorted an old ox-wagon of the pioneer days of the veld to Government House, just as the fleet of royal cars was about to leave, and induced the Prince to jump on board. This he did with spontaneous good humour, mingling with the boisterous students as they were drawn through the streets to the University by a team of horned oxen. The escapade became front-page news in the press under such headlines as THE PRINCE ENJOYS A STUDENT RAG, THE DEMOCRATIC PRINCE, THE PRINCE OF SOUTH AFRICANS, and instantly caught the imagination of the people of Capetown.

A more arduous challenge confronted the Prince in his three-months' journey upcountry into the various states and protectorates of the Union. He travelled ten thousand miles in a special train which also carried not twenty-five polo ponies, as in India, but two cows to provide fresh milk for his party. He met dogged Boer farmers of long memory and veterans who had fought the British in the bitter Boer Wars. For the first time he heard tell of their battles, familiar to him in the schoolroom, from the Dutch side—horrific tales of British concentration camps and the burning of Boer farmsteads. At Ladysmith, the town of the famous siege, a Nationalist minister pulled up his trouser-leg to show him a large scar, and recalled, "Sir, you British put nine bullets into me that day!" Another minister implacably refused to be seen riding with the Prince in Johannesburg, while a third, educated at Oxford, declared to him coldly that he could never forgive the British for their "wanton attack" on the two Boer republics. When the Prince suggested that time might heal his people's resentment, the minister answered emphatically, "No, Sir. Never."

None of these memories however prevented the Dutch settlers from showing him warm hospitality. Columns of burly Dutch farmers would ride out from their "dorps," the farming towns of the veld, to meet his train, riding shaggy horses as the Boer commandos had done in their raids on the British, but no longer, as then, with a Bible under one arm and a rifle under the other. On the outskirts of Oudtshoorn the Prince, on an impulse, borrowed a spare horse and, in his ordinary lounge suit and a soft hat, galloped at the head of them to the town recreation ground. The crowd of twenty-five thousand awaiting him looked on at first with bewilderment, then, on recognizing the Prince, with vociferous cheers of delight. Thenceforward the Prince took to alighting from his train and riding into other towns in this commando fashion. Here, the Dutch people saw with delight, was a sportsman. They cheered him because, as one of them said, "We know a man when we see one."

The Prince rode into Bloemfontein, a hotbed of nationalism, at the head of a commando twelve hundred strong. Over the last mile, which was on asphalt, he tried to check the pace, for the sake of his horse. But, as he remarked afterwards, "There was nothing doing. It was just hell-for-leather." Then, from the saddle of his panting charger, he addressed the burghers in Afrikaans, as he had addressed the Indians in Urdu. As a local Member of Parliament said of him, "It is not the royalty of the person which has got us, it is the personality of the royalty."

Stories rang round the Union of his simplicity, his humour, his faculty for laughing at himself. Here he played the ukulele with a serenading party of Kaffirs and Hottentots. There he danced with a poor actress, playing Prince Charming to her Cinderella as he said, "I'm on the stage too, in a way. I've been a showman all my life." Once a mayor, mixing up the notes of his speech of welcome, paused in embarrassment after reading, "Not only do we welcome Your Royal Highness as the representative of His Majesty the King but . . ." The Prince, knowing the formula, at once prompted him in a whisper, "We welcome you for *yourself*."

One evening, on the royal pilot train, he joined in a sing-song, borrowing an unfamiliar jazz instrument from a pressman, which he started to play. After he had stumbled through "John Brown's Body," there was a pause, which he broke with an attempt at another melody. As the Prince got the hang of the instrument it was suddenly recognized: "God Bless the Prince of Wales!"—the song which had been greeting him shrilly from the lips of thousands of schoolchildren, all over South Africa. The company joined in, and for a few more bars the Prince continued. Then he exploded into laughter and, holding up his hands, cried, "For Heaven's sake, that's enough!"

In the native areas he became once more the son of the "Great White

On his tour through Zululand.

King." Zulu, Basuto, Kaffir, and Bantu tribesmen who had fought the British
and each other until calmed by the *Pax Britannica,* travelled hundreds of miles
to set eyes on him and see for themselves whether he was "for our hearts as well as
for our words." They rallied before him in their tens of thousands, reviving
scenes of barbaric splendour reminiscent of the works of Rider Haggard. They
danced before him and recited odes and sang chants in their resonant, deep-
chested voices. They showered him with gifts of assagais, cow-hide shields, elephant tusks, receiving silver-topped Malacca canes in return. Striving to live up
to their colourful costumes, he wore the full-dress uniform of the Brigade of

Guards, his scarlet tunic glittering with decorations and medals and with the broad blue ribbon of the Order of the Garter across it.

"There is only one House," shouted the Zulus, "and that is the King's House! Thou whose loveliness surpasses the loveliness of butterflies . . . we bow down to our adorned ankles before thee in homage. . . . We thought that we were conquered, that we were crushed and finished, but we have lived to learn that it is not the British way. Having experienced the mildness of British rule, we rejoice the more because it subdued us."

A Basuto chief, near to death, croaked, "I rejoice as old Simeon of the Holy Scriptures rejoiced when he was privileged to set eyes upon the Lord Jesus." The Prince responded in practical fashion: "Today you live in peace and prosperity under British rule. The King continues to watch over you with fatherly care. You will show yourselves worthy of his protection by listening to the words of the officers appointed to guide and instruct you. They will educate you to bring up your children to make best use of your land, to free your cattle from disease and to restrict their number so as not to tire out the land."

The Prince's last destination was South America. Crossing the South Atlantic, the *Repulse* put in at St. Helena, where, mindful of a willow at Windsor grown from a tree which had shaded Napoleon, he planted an olive-tree beside his empty grave. In Buenos Aires "God bless the Prince of Wales!" gave place to *"Vivace el Principe de Gales!"* while flocks of doves, tinted red, white, and blue, fluttered down from the rooftops to greet him. Here a different assignment confronted him. For the first time in royal history, a Prince was to be employed as an ambassador for British trade. The war had weakened Britain's position in the Argentine market, where American competition was strong, and it was hoped that the Prince of Wales's popularity would rebound to his country's commercial advantage.

That it did so Bonar Law, who had succeeded Lloyd George as Prime Minister, was to testify: "Not only have the Prince's Empire missions been followed with great interest by the whole of His Majesty's subjects, but also the whole civilized world has intelligently observed the experiment of the British Government in sending out this young member of the House of Windsor to gain trade for themselves and their dominions. Napoleon once sneered at England for being a nation of shopkeepers, and in truth even fifty years ago prosaic trade seemed to be a poor thing compared with the romance of Courts. Despite the many-sided excellences of the late King Edward, he was not what you would call a commercial man. King George is more of a business man, but for sheer commercial brilliance the Prince easily overshadows even His Majesty."

The Prince's aptitude for business was such that he was to be sent on another visit to South America five years later, to open a British trade exhibition at Buenos Aires. To the delight of the Argentinians he delivered his opening speech in Spanish, and received a telegram of felicitations from Mr. Baldwin, by then Prime Minister and a man not normally so free with his praises as his predecessors:

WELL DONE, SIR. MY WARMEST AND MOST RESPECTFUL
CONGRATULATIONS ON YOUR SPEECH. SPANISH PUNDITS
DELIGHTED WITH YOUR PRONUNCIATION.

The Prince did his job thoroughly, interviewing the financiers and industrialists of the various republics, inspecting factories, poking around department stores and wholesale emporia, comparing South American products to those of his own country and collecting samples of them to show to manufacturers at home. On his return he was apostrophized in a House of Commons debate as "the greatest commercial traveller and the most powerful advertising medium that the world has known." Later he gave a straight-from-the-shoulder talk to a large meeting of businessmen in Manchester, criticizing their commercial methods and insisting, "We are supplying the goods of yesterday while our foreign competitors are supplying the goods of today. . . . But I am convinced that by a closer study of these markets, and by the exercise of more imagination, we can go one better than our competitors and supply the goods of tomorrow."

Meanwhile, in October 1925, the Prince arrived home after his main series of tours. In six years he had visited forty-five different countries and colonies, covering—before the age of air travel—a total distance of a hundred and fifty thousand miles, the equivalent of six journeys round the world. Lord Curzon described him as "the most travelled Prince since the Emperor Hadrian."

In his own estimation, he had been able "to savour something of the atmosphere of hundreds of different communities. . . . I could have qualified as a self-contained encyclopaedia on railway gauges, national anthems, statistics, local customs and dishes, and the political affiliations of a hundred mayors. I know the gold output of the Rand, the storage capacity of the grain elevators at Winnipeg, and the wool export of Australia. . . . The number of memorial trees I planted, if they have survived the vicissitudes of climate and the depredations of man, must today constitute a substantial forest. And the number of public buildings and institutions whose foundation-stones I laid would comprise, could they be brought together, a sizable city."

The education of the Prince had been completed, it was said, on the trade-routes of the world. And in the course of it he discovered "how much of the world's hard work, the dirty work, was being done by a handful of my countrymen." He was the last King to have traversed the British Empire with its component parts still intact. In so doing, he did the Empire a major service at this turning-point of its history. The impact of his personality upon it was both a

Dressed in some of the many roles he played as the Empire's "best salesman."

stiffener and a solvent, crystallizing the loyalty of the English-speaking dominions and, in the others, calming forces of disruption at a moment when their loyalty was beginning to wane.

For this achievement alone he is likely to rank, in the estimation of posterity, as a great Prince of Wales—probably the greatest in the history of Britain.

Chapter VII

The Prince of Wales was now thirty-one. He had given the best part of his youth to his country. While his contemporaries, returning home after five years of war, had been able to settle down, building up homes, marrying wives, founding families, and generally establishing their personal lives on a permanent basis, the Prince, globe-trotting in the national and imperial interest, had been condemned to a life that was inherently restless. He could never feel himself rooted, as the friends around him were. Willy-nilly he had become, as he put it, a rolling stone that had difficulty in coming to rest.

Between tours and afterwards he had plenty of work to do at home. In the course of his public duties he toured the greater part of England, Scotland, and Wales, getting to know his own country as he had got to know its dominions. He visited coal mines, factories, hospitals, educational establishments. He inspected military units. He opened bridges and roads and municipal projects. He patronized sporting events. He presided over institutions devoted to charitable enterprises. He attended innumerable public dinners, in the midst of what he called "the decorated circus" of after-dinner speakers and celebrities in white ties and tails. While other men might be chained to their desks, the Prince, as he jested, was chained to the banquet table.

But, as an antidote to these chores, he was free to enjoy the "bright magic" of that post-war age which was to become known as the "Roaring Twenties." It was an age when youth was seeking its freedom, reacting against the conventions and traditions of the past to find its individual self and express it without inhibition. In the social world it was an age of gaiety and pleasure, of change and experiment, yet still of transition, thus benefiting from the best of two worlds. For

Back in London after four long voyages, the debonair Prince between public duties enjoyed some of the relaxations of the "Roaring Twenties."

The Crown Prince of Japan visits the City of London. Left to right: the Duke of York, the Crown Prince, the Lord Mayor of London, the Prince of Wales.

another decade to come the aristocracy was to maintain some sway over society in its great London houses and stately country homes.

The Prince of Wales, fresh from Australia, relished especially the glittering "London Season" of 1921, when the Household Troops at last discarded their wartime khaki for the traditional full-dress scarlet tunics and bearskin caps, and the guests of blue-blooded hostesses ate dinners once more off gold and silver plate, served by footmen in family livery, with knee-breeches. Nevertheless man-

136

ners were relaxing, and the doors were opening to admit a circle distinctly wider than that of their Edwardian and Victorian forebears. Outside London the great sporting pageants of the Derby, the Ascot Races, the regatta at Cowes, shone as brightly and, within their Royal Enclosures, as exclusively as ever before.

But the true essence of the Roaring Twenties was informal amusement. This was the "Golden Age" of the cocktail party, the restaurant, the night club, the floor show. In this new society the Prince of Wales, often to the displeasure of King George, fell naturally into the role of a leader of fashion, much as his grandfather, always to the displeasure of Queen Victoria, had done in his own generation. Nightly he was to be seen escaping from some more formal function to sup and dance to the new jazz bands in such fashionable resorts as the Embassy Club—"that Buckingham Palace of night clubs"—the Kit-Cat, and the Café de Paris, with its "champagne and chandeliers," which his patronage helped to save at a time when it was faced with a deficit of some thousands of pounds.

The bar of Mayfair's popular Kit-Cat Club.

ABOVE: With Thomas Hardy and his wife.

BELOW: After an international polo match at Hurlingham, the Prince of Wales, dressed in a top hat and tails, watches while the team is presented to King Alfonso of Spain.

The Prince, to the delight and profit of the tailors and haberdashers of London, became an arbiter too of male fashion. His equerries would await with curiosity his morning appearances, asking one another, "What will he be wearing this time?" His clothes became "news" in the daily press, to the point even of foreshadowing a new fashion when he once appeared, having changed in a hurry, in turned-up trousers with his morning-coat, or again, on a cold evening, with a pullover under his dinner-jacket. Always he had fretted at the constrictions of dress, symbolic of other constrictions, which his family's conventional habits prescribed. Other males fretted too, in this free-and-easy age, and they were quick to follow his lead in the direction of sartorial freedom and comfort.

ABOVE: In plus-fours, spats, cutaway jacket, and patterned socks. RIGHT: With Al Smith, Governor of New York, at the opening of the bridge at Niagara Falls.

The Prince in particular led a rebellion against starch. His father still wore a boiled shirt, white tie, and tails, even when he was dining quietly at home, and he expected his sons, when they dined with him, to do the same. This convention still prevailed in the "great houses." But the Prince, when he went out on his own, would have none of it. First the tails disappeared, and the dinner-jacket, worn by his grandfather only for small private dinners, became, under his auspices, the normal evening attire, whether in private or in public. Gradually the stiff shirt was replaced by a soft shirt, the stiff collar by a soft collar, and both by a collar-attached soft shirt. The waistcoat at first became backless, a fashion which he greatly encouraged, and finally withered away with the birth of the double-breasted dinner-jacket.

The Prince's softening-up process in costume extended to sports clothes, when plus-fours and sweaters took the place, on the golf course, of breeches and Norfolk jackets. When the Prince played himself in, as Captain of the Royal and Ancient Golf Club at St. Andrews, his indifferent first shot to the sound of a gun, before a large crowd, prompted the local headline, WHAT THE PRINCE SAID

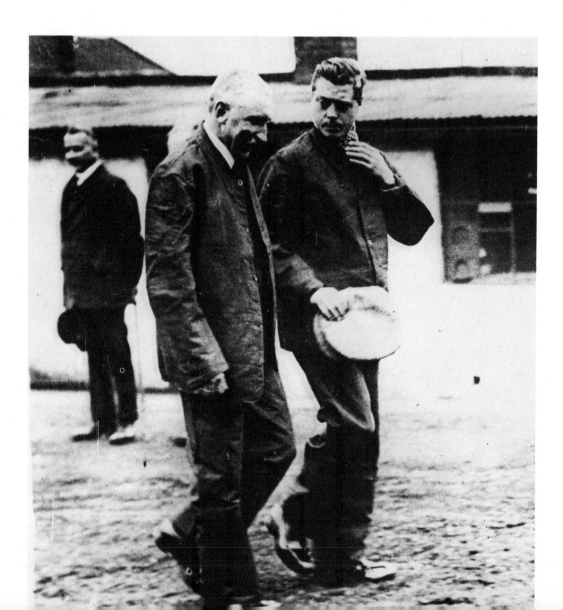

OPPOSITE: On a visit to Whitehaven, in Cumberland, the Prince of Wales, dressed as a miner, inspects the Haig Collieries. ABOVE: Reviewing disabled ex-servicemen workers at the British Legion Poppy Factory. The Prince was accompanied by eight Canadian holders of the Victoria Cross.

With his mother and father in the royal carriage.

WHEN HE TOPPED HIS DRIVE. But his multi-coloured Fair Isle sweater, with its jigsaw of patterns, launched a fashion, bringing much relief to the Hebridean crofters who knitted these garments.

Sport was the Prince's main recreation. "Had I been of a studious nature," he wrote of himself, "I might have cultivated an amateur's interest in literature or listened to Sir Ernest Rutherford discourse on the splitting of the atom. But it so happened that I preferred physical to intellectual exercise." It became with him almost a fetish. On his tours he often wore out his staff by his insistence on a "good sweat" at the end of each day. After a long and tiring bout of official functions, they would return ready for a doze in an arm-chair and a drink in the evening. But the Prince would say, "Well, that's over. Come on, let's have a game of golf before dinner." Travelling across continents he would often stop the Royal train, put on a pair of shorts and a couple of sweaters, and set off on a steady double of some miles down the track, with an equerry panting in his wake and the train moving on slowly to keep pace with him.

In India he had kept fit by playing polo. Now at home he was able to return to his favourite pastime of fox-hunting; and he took also to riding in point-to-point races and steeplechases. He became indeed the first heir to the Throne

142

to win a steeplechase. Each winter he took apartments at Craven Lodge, a hunting club, well-equipped with stables, at Melton Mowbray in Leicestershire, in the heart of the English hunting shires. Here the smart set mixed, in pursuit of the fox across undulating well-fenced grassland, with the landed gentry, the sturdy yeomen farmers, and a strong contingent of American and other overseas horsemen. An outstanding personality among them was Squire "Algy" Burnaby, the Master of the Quorn, who would keep his hard-riding field in control with such caustic injunctions as "Come back, young feller. Who the hell do you think you are, the Prince of Wales?"

The Prince was an adventurous rider, who had his fair share of falls, whether in the hunting-field or on the steeplechase course. These tumbles were no more than the normal hazards of sport, for the Prince was a good enough rider, with an excellent stable of horses. But they were magnified by the press into headline "news." Wisecracks about the Prince falling off his horse rivalled the popular music-hall jokes.

But a more serious accident, when he fell on his head, got concussion, and was in bed for some weeks, aroused public concern. Following a question in Parliament the Prince received a letter from the Prime Minister, begging him, in view of his indispensability to the nation, to refrain from taking such risks. More important was an admonitory letter from his father, with a strongly worded request that he give up riding in steeplechases and point-to-point races. And to this he eventually acceded, selling his stable of horses and concentrating more on what the King, hard to please, called "his tiresome golf."

The relations between the Prince of Wales and his father had never been smooth, and as he grew older they did not grow smoother. Despite the Prince's age, the King persistently refused to give him specific State duties or to initiate him into Government business. He was never present at audiences. He saw no official papers, except Foreign Office telegrams relevant to his missions abroad. He was discouraged by his father from contacts with ministers. He lived in a political vacuum, which gave a certain unreality to his public duties and his responsibilities as heir to the Throne. He was in much the same predicament as his grandfather, King Edward VII, had been as Prince of Wales, a royal figurehead excluded by his mother from the affairs of State.

King George V moreover was a man of fixed habits and views. Essentially a Victorian still, he disliked change and abhorred the ways of the young generation. His constant refrain was: "We never did that in the olden days"—and this applied to much that his son did. Night clubs, to the King, were haunts of vice and crime. The short-skirted, shingle-haired "new woman" filled him with distaste. "He disapproved," in the words of his son, "of Soviet Russia, painted fingernails, women who smoked in public, cocktails, frivolous hats, American

The Prince on horseback competing in the Duchess of Rutland's cup races at the Belvoir Hunt cross-country contest, Barrowby.

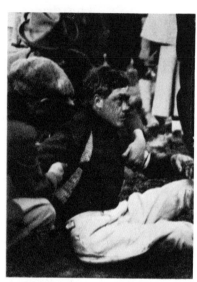

After a fall.

On the way to the post.

"The first heir to the throne to win a steeplechase" takes a jump—and (BELOW) another toss.

jazz, and the growing habit of going away for week-ends." While the Prince was in South America, the King once wrote to the Queen, "I see David continues to dance every night and most of the night too. What a pity they should telegraph it every day, people who don't know, will begin to think that he is either mad or the biggest rake in Europe, such a pity."

The Prince himself, belonging as he did to a generation of change, was an inquisitive young man, eager for experience, and ready to "try everything once." Since he worked hard, he considered himself entitled to play hard. But the King, leading a sedentary, conservative life, thought his son "terribly restless," and Queen Mary agreed with him. Puzzled that her son did not share her own tastes, she regarded him with an affection which, in the words of her biographer, was "always mingled with apprehension and surprise."

The King was especially appalled by reports of the Prince's social pursuits in America, which he visited for a second time, *en route* for his ranch in Alberta, to play polo and watch the international matches. The press featured his visit under such headlines as PRINCE GETS IN WITH MILKMAN . . . OH! WHO'LL ASK H.R.H. WHAT HE WEARS ASLEEP? . . . HERE HE IS, GIRLS—THE MOST ELIGIBLE BACHELOR YET UNCAUGHT! In vain did the Prince, confronted later by his father with a sheaf of such press-cuttings, try to convince him that no Americans took them too seriously and that the bark of the American press was far worse than its bite. The King replied severely, "If this vulgarity represents the American attitude towards people in our position, little purpose would be served in your exposing yourself again to this kind of treatment." Thenceforward he "privately broke off relations between America and the members of his family," and for many years the Prince and his brothers were effectively discouraged from visiting the United States.

A fundamental source of unease to the King was his son's reluctance, despite all parental hints, to marry—to take his chance in what the Prince called the "grab bag" of the royal marriage market. This his father had done with the happiest results, finding that "wedding bells were the true answer to a young man's restlessness." But the market had shrunk since King George's youth, with the dwindling of the European monarchical dynasties. As a result the Royal Family had now started to marry in their own country, choosing partners from aristocratic but non-royal families. To the gratification of the British public, Princess Mary, the Prince's only sister, had been married to Lord Lascelles, the heir to the Earl of Harewood, while his brother the Duke of York had married Lady Elizabeth Bowes-Lyon, a daughter of the Earl of Strathmore. The Prince of Wales, it was generally hoped, would follow their example, seeking the hand of some English girl of good family.

But, here today and gone tomorrow, his personal attachments were forever

146

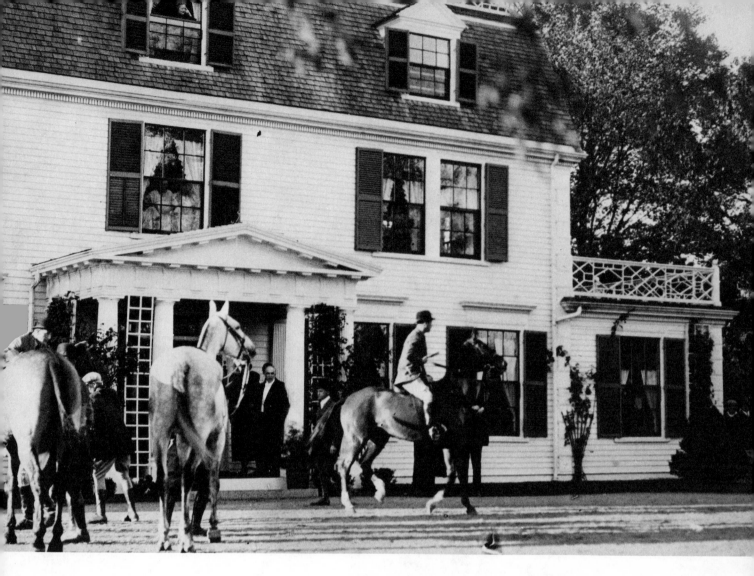

At the Myopia Hunt, Hamilton, Massachusetts.

interrupted, his affections seldom had the time to mature on a permanent basis. He had made up his mind that, when he came to marry, his choice would be dictated "not by considerations of State but by my own heart." The idea of a loveless marriage was repugnant to him, and no eligible bride had yet "stirred my blood or been sentimentally drawn to me." "This is not to suggest," he afterwards wrote, "that my emotions during these youthful years of travel and intermingling had escaped being moved. There had been moments of tenderness, even enchantment, without which a Princely existence would have been almost intolerable. But in so far as marriage was concerned, I was determined not to be hurried. Therefore, my life went along pervaded, as I realize now, by a sense of incompleteness and inner discontent."

What King George did not know was that, on his arrival in New York, a young female reporter had inquired of him, "Would you marry an American gal if you fell in love with one?" His answer was lost in the general laughter of the newspapermen. It was "Yes."

147

Chapter
VIII

*T*he Prince of Wales had yet to find a wife. But in 1930 he at last found a home. Hitherto he had lived in bachelor quarters in York House, St. James's, which was also his office. But he was a man who loved the country, feeling caged after the briefest of spells in the turmoil of London, and for some years past he had been renting small country houses from which to play golf and enjoy an open-air life. Now there fell vacant a royal "Grace and Favour" residence named Fort Belvedere, on the edge of Windsor Great Park. At the Prince's request, the King handed it over to him, remarking, "What could you possibly want that queer old place for? Those damned week-ends, I suppose." Thus the rolling stone began to come to rest.

The "queer old place" was an eighteenth-century house, restored and enlarged in a castellated style by Wyatville, the architect of the gothicized Windsor Castle, to house a favourite, it was said, of King George IV. The Prince set himself with energy and imagination to modernize the Fort, cutting down yew-trees and shrubberies to let in the light, enlisting his week-end guests as manual labourers to help hack away the undergrowth, transplant shrubs, and clear paths through the woodlands around it. A new and essentially English interest was thus born in the Prince, to the exclusion of fox-hunting and even, to some extent, golf—that of gardening. With his own hands he created a garden, planting herbaceous borders, mowing hay, and building a rockery with cascades from the neighbouring lake of Virginia Water. The Prince came to love his new home, which became for him "a peaceful, almost enchanted anchorage," offering a refuge from the cares of his public life.

At the same time he redecorated York House in London. Here he now provided quarters for his favourite brother, Prince George, later the Duke of Kent, who had just left the Navy, and with whom he had developed a happy and intimate relationship. A few years earlier they had made two journeys together, to Spain as the guests of King Alfonso, and, once more, to Canada—this time in

The Prince receives an ovation at the Crystal Palace, London.

the company of Mr. Stanley Baldwin, who was destined to play a fateful part in the Prince's future. The Prince had not lost his wanderlust, and in the following year he went to East Africa with his brother Harry, the Duke of Gloucester, to try his hand at big game shooting. But while he was on safari in the wilds of Tanganyika, King George fell dangerously ill at Buckingham Palace, with an abscess in the lung which affected his heart.

A cruiser was sent to fetch the Prince home. Mussolini sent his private train to rush him across Europe. When he landed at Brindisi the news of his father was better, and his brother the Duke of York, in a letter to him, was able to joke: "There is a lovely story going about which emanated from the East End that the reason of your rushing home is that in the event of anything happening to Papa I am going to bag the Throne in your absence!!!! Just like the Middle Ages . . ."

The King recovered but the illness had weakened him; his convalescence was long, and for some time the Prince of Wales was called upon to take over a number of his duties. He held levées on his behalf—royal receptions in the

York House, in St. James's Palace, the Prince of Wales' London home. The tower and gateway were built in the reign of Henry VIII.

Fort Belvedere, in Windsor Great Park, became the Prince's country residence in 1930.

OVERLEAF: At Ealing Studios, for the shooting of a film starring Owen Nares and Betty Stockfield.

Throne Room of St. James's Palace, at which diplomats, ministers, high officials, Army officers, and other personages paid their respects to the Crown. He escorted his mother at Courts, formal full-dress presentation ceremonies in the ballroom of Buckingham Palace.

But as the years went by the Prince, in his public life, became more and more absorbed in the grave social problems which confronted the new Britain. The inter-war years were an era of chronic unemployment and of discontent among the working classes, which precipitated the General Strike of 1926. This might have led to a revolutionary crisis had it not been defeated by the voluntary effort of the middle and upper classes, who forsook their jobs and their homes to keep the country's essential services running. It gave added point and impetus to the Prince's self-chosen mission of seeing for himself the conditions in the industrial areas, and doing all he could to alleviate distress.

During the years that followed, culminating in the world depression of 1931, when the number of unemployed rose above two-and-a-half million and hunger marches from the provinces caused angry street demonstrations in London, he saw many grim sights in his tours around the country: ". . . throngs of

The Prince arriving for the opening of the Shakespeare Memorial Theatre, Stratford-on-Avon, April 23, 1932.

idle men everywhere, with nowhere to go. In town after town, village after village, one would come upon dejected groups aimlessly milling in the streets or standing about outside the labour exchanges and in front of the pubs they lacked the means to patronize. The saddest fact of all was that tens of thousands of these unemployed had come to judge themselves useless and unwanted." His human sympathy touched and his social conscience aroused by what he saw, he became, as no royal personage had been before him, "the Prince of the People."

He toured areas where pits had shut down and whole communities were on the dole. He visited soup-kitchens, watching the hungry being fed, moved to compassion by the sight of a workless young man with no shirt under his jacket. He went into the poor cottages of unemployed miners, here comforting the widow of one who had died in penury that morning, there holding the hand of a woman in the pangs of child-birth. Sometimes he was received in sullen silence. But gradually the working people came to realize that he was on their side, that he was trying to get something done for them in practical terms, that the Government was less indifferent than they had supposed to their plight. He associated himself in particular with the workingmen's clubs, whose drabness he sought to relieve.

Back in London, he badgered his friends and the general public to contribute to the Lord Mayor's Fund for distressed miners, of which he was patron. In a Christmas broadcast he aroused the admiration of Mr. Cook, the "raving wrecker" from the Left, who had inspired the miners' strike in 1926, and who now addressed him: "I was with two Communist friends, and when your name

154

was announced to speak on behalf of the Miners' Fund, they undoubtedly scoffed. But they listened to what you had to say, and when you finished, with tears in their eyes, they put their hands in their pockets and gave what money they had on them to the fund."

Appealing over the radio for recruits for voluntary social services, the Prince told a touching tale:

"A committee meeting was in progress just before Christmas in a small club in a very poor neighbourhood of London. The members, mostly unemployed or casually employed, with large families and living in two rooms on a very small weekly income, had already contributed towards a Christmas party for their own children. Further suggestions were called for by the chairman and one man got up and proposed that

At Oxford University for the opening of the new extension to the Taylor Institution. The Prince is accompanied by the Vice-Chancellor.

another subscription should be raised amongst the members for another party for the children of the people in the neighbourhood who were even poorer than themselves, and who had not the benefit of the club and its canteen. This was done."

Visiting housing estates which were all too slowly replacing the Liverpool slums, he discussed with Lord Derby, a man of influence in the neighbourhood, the Government's lack of initiative. On an impulse the Prince invited him to a dinner at York House, together with others who shared his views. Here they met the Prime Minister and other ministers and discussed around the table, in critical terms, the official housing policy. Further than this he could not go, since his prerogative, as Prince of Wales, was limited to the power of suggestion. But as Duke of Cornwall he had property of his own, not only in Cornwall but in a slum district of London. Here he planned, with the advice of an architect friend, to develop a vacant site with mass-produced low-rent housing. He was prevented from doing so only by the fact that the London County Council had already acquired the site from the Duchy for a building project of its own, and refused to release it.

In order to get around the country more quickly, to stimulate the British aviation industry, and to test his own prowess at this newest of all sports, the Prince took to flying—this time, rather surprisingly, with the consent of his father. He obtained his pilot's licence, but, once he had done so, did not normally pilot his own plane.

Such was the Prince of Wales's public life—that of his prescribed royal duties on the one hand and, on the other, that of the task, on behalf of the unemployed, which he had prescribed for himself. His private life meanwhile had become transformed by the contentments of his new home, The Fort. Within its walls and in its garden he created an atmosphere which was personal, informal, and wholly relaxed. He called it "my Get-Away-from-People house." For here he got away from family, household, public personages, official contacts, and social acquaintances, and collected around him a small circle of friends of his own choosing. One of these was an American woman, Wallis Warfield by birth, who was married to an Englishman, Ernest Simpson. Their relationship, developing and flourishing in the easy atmosphere of The Fort, was to have fateful results for the Prince's future and that of his country.

As president of the Westminster Hospital, the Prince of Wales visits the Old Westminster Fair and Market in the Dean's Yard.

PRECEDING PAGES: After obtaining his pilot's license, the Prince gets ready for a reviewing flight from the aircraft carrier *Courageous*.

The Prince of Wales and Prince George driving to Crathie Church near Balmoral in Scotland. OPPOSITE: Their niece Princess Elizabeth (later Queen Elizabeth II) at the age of four.

In November 1934, his brother the Duke of Kent (formerly Prince George) married Princess Marina of Greece. In the wedding group, from left to right: Princess Catherine of Greece, Princess Eugénie of Greece, Prince of Wales, Lady Iris Mountbatten, the bride and bridegroom, Princess Irene of Greece, the Duke of York, Grand Duchess Kyra of Russia, Princess Juliana of Holland. Seated: Lady Mary Cambridge and Princess Elizabeth of York, the present Queen Elizabeth.

RIGHT: The Duchess of Kent a few months after the wedding. The marriage ended in tragedy eight years later when the Duke of Kent was killed in an R.A.F. bomber crash. OVERLEAF: A garden party in the grounds of Buckingham Palace, given by King George and Queen Mary.

ABOVE: Wallis Warfield's mother, Alice Montague, at the turn of the century. RIGHT: Her father, Teackle Wallis Warfield, who died when Wallis was five months old.

Wallis Simpson was a Southerner, of colonial stock, from Baltimore, Maryland. During the war, at the age of twenty, she had been married to a lieutenant in the United States Navy, Winfield Spencer. The marriage broke up after the war, while he was stationed in China. Her present husband had been reared in New York but was now in business in London, where he had made his home.

166

The Simpsons first met the Prince of Wales in the autumn of 1930, spending a week-end with Thelma Lady Furness, a mutual American-born friend, at her country house near Melton Mowbray.

Dark, active, and slim, Mrs. Simpson was a woman of charm and vitality, rather than beauty, and the Prince responded to her frankness of speech, her quickness of humour and sense of fun. Their friendship grew slowly over a period of three years. In the summer of 1931, arrayed in the traditional Court feathers and train, she was presented at Court at Buckingham Palace. As she curtsied to the King and Queen the Prince, standing behind their gilt thrones,

BELOW: Wallis Warfield as a girl with her first pet, "Bully," given to her by her stepfather, John Freeman Rasin. RIGHT: As a debutante in 1915. Sixteen years later Wallis, as Mrs. Ernest Simpson, was presented at Court at Buckingham Palace.

The Simpsons' drawing room in their London flat at Bryanston Court.

was "struck by the grace of her carriage and the natural dignity of her movements." When they met afterwards at supper with Lord and Lady Furness, he admired her dress. "But, Sir," she replied, "I understood that you thought we all looked ghastly!" The Prince was taken aback, then smiled and said, "I had no idea my voice carried so far."

Acquaintanceship ripened into friendship as Wallis Simpson revealed to him, as his women friends seldom did, a serious interest in his job. At dinner one evening at the Dorchester Hotel, she encouraged him to tell her of the day he had spent, visiting workingmen's clubs in the industrial towns and villages of Yorkshire, and of his social schemes for the unemployed. He talked to her of a new Council of Social Service, of which she had read in the newspapers and, above the noise of the orchestra, replied at length to her questions, which expressed a genuine curiosity about such social problems and about his working

168

Wallis Simpson in the early nineteen-thirties.

life as Prince of Wales. He came to respect her as a woman of independent out-look—"one of the happier outcomes," as he put it, "of the events of 1776." He came to enjoy in particular her forthright way of expressing views which often disagreed with his own and gave him a welcome chance for argument. This was an unfamiliar stimulus for a Prince used to the reticent ways of a courtly entourage.

Their sense of companionship grew—at The Fort, where the Simpsons became regular week-end guests, and where she often advised him on household arrangements; and in their London flat where he took to dropping in for a quiet evening. While her husband was in America, she stayed with him, escorted by her aunt, at Biarritz, and accompanied him on a Mediterranean cruise in the yacht of a mutual friend. They went skiing together, with a party, at Kitzbühel, and afterwards visited Vienna and Budapest. Another summer, they cruised along the Mediterranean coast and revisited Central Europe. Meanwhile the

The dining room at Bryanston Court.

The Prince and Mrs. Simpson in Vienna.

Prince's friends took to inviting them together to informal dinners in London. He introduced her to his father and mother at the wedding reception of Prince George and Princess Marina of Greece. With her husband she attended a State ball at Buckingham Palace. As she danced with the Prince she fancied that the King's eyes rested upon her with a searching look.

Gradually Wallis Simpson came to mean more and more to the Prince, until the moment at which he realized that his heart was profoundly engaged. "Presently and imperceptibly," he afterwards wrote, "the hope formed that one day I might be able to share my life with her, just how I did not know." For the first time in his life he had fallen seriously in love; and as he had resolved to marry only for love the question of ultimate marriage with Mrs. Simpson now entered his mind. He was fully aware of its constitutional difficulties. The Royal Marriages Act of 1772 placed marriages of Princes of the Blood Royal under the control of the Sovereign and ultimately of Parliament. The King had the power to veto his choice of a wife, and in this case would almost certainly do so. Sooner

In May 1935 King George V
and Queen Mary celebrated
the twenty-fifth year of their
reign. During the week of
ceremonies, the Prince received his mother at Windsor.
The Duke of Gloucester rode
from London with the Queen.

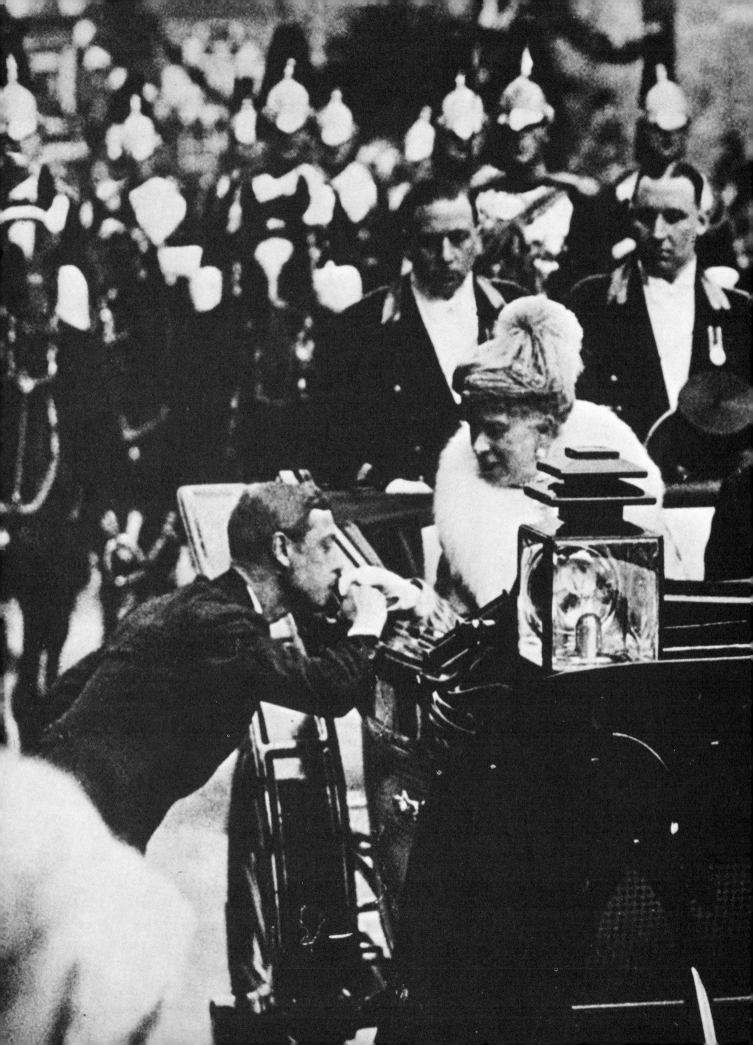

OPPOSITE: The King and Queen drive down Fleet Street in their Silver Jubilee Procession. ABOVE: The Prince, the Duke of Gloucester, and Queen Maud of Norway.

OVERLEAF: The Royal Family gather on the balcony at Buckingham Palace to receive the ovation of the crowds after the Jubilee Thanksgiving Service in St. Paul's Cathedral.

or later he intended to broach the matter with his father. But this was hard, at the moment, to do.

For King George was nearing seventy, and his health was steadily failing as, in the summer of 1935, he entered the twenty-fifth year of his reign. His Silver Jubilee was celebrated by a Thanksgiving Service in St. Paul's Cathedral, for which he afterwards broadcast his own message of thanks to his people. This was followed by a week of exacting public ceremonies, with processional drives through London in which the people were able to show their reverence for the Crown as an emblem of unity and continuity in a rapidly dissolving world, and

BELOW: Stanley Baldwin, Conservative Prime Minister, delivers a political speech in England while trouble brews in Hitler's Germany and Mussolini's Italy.

ABOVE RIGHT: The historic first meeting of Hitler and Mussolini, in Venice, 1934. Between the two leaders is Ulrich von Hassel (later executed as one of the instigators of the bomb attack on Hitler). Next to Mussolini (with arm raised) is Count Cerutti, and to the right, Herman von Neurath. OPPOSITE: Emperor Haile Selassie with King Victor Emmanuel III and the Italian Crown Prince. The Italians annexed Abyssinia (Ethiopia) in May 1936.

their respect for King George as the personal embodiment of those British virtues and ideals which they cherished the most. It left the King overtired, and the events of that autumn were such as to keep him busy and tire him still further. At home there was a General Election, which returned the Conservatives to power. Abroad a world crisis mounted as Mussolini invaded Abyssinia.

The Duke of Gloucester and his bride, at Buckingham Palace, November 1935.

At Christmas the King gathered his family around him at Sandringham. All felt that this might be his last Christmas and endeavoured to make it a happy one. The third generation was prominent in the persons of the Duke of York's children, Princess Elizabeth and Princess Margaret, romping around the twenty-foot tree. The Duke of Gloucester had lately married Lady Alice Montagu-Douglas-Scott, and the King had written in his diary, "Now all the children are married but David." The Prince of Wales, seeing them thus married and secure in their family lives as he was not, became aware of his own loneliness. The conflict within him between public and private self was approaching its crisis. But this was not the moment to discuss his intentions with his father.

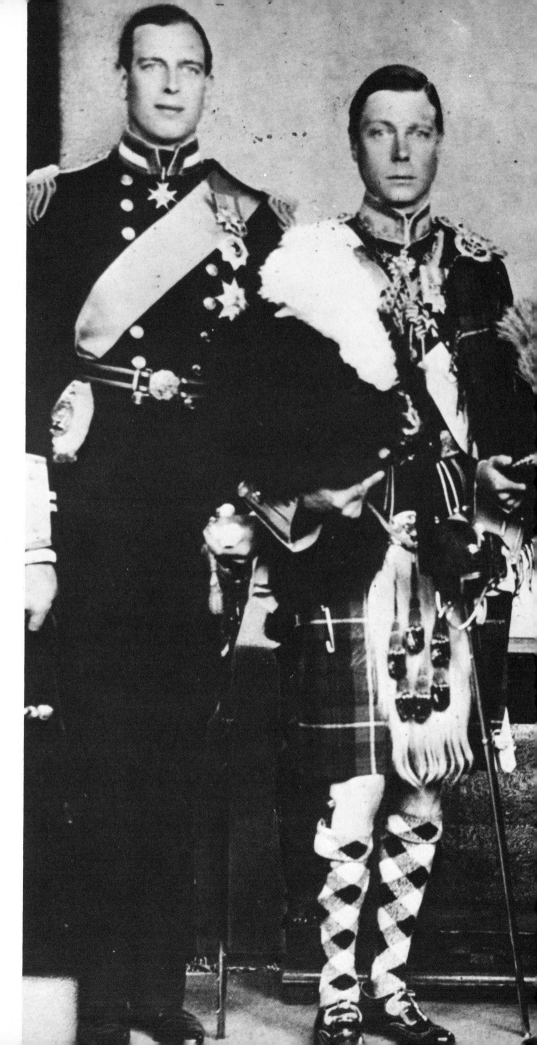

Four royal brothers: the Duke of Kent, the Prince of Wales, the Duke of York (who was to succeed him as King), and the Duke of Gloucester.

That moment never came. Early in the New Year the King fell gravely ill. The family reassembled at Sandringham, this time around his death-bed. His life, in the words of his doctor broadcast over the radio, was "moving peacefully towards its close." A Council of State, consisting of the Queen and their four sons, was formed to take over his duties. Just before midnight, on January 20, 1936, he died.

The Prince of Wales was now King. To his embarrassment his mother took his hand by the bedside and kissed it in homage. His brother George did the same. Next day, in the Banqueting Hall at St. James's Palace, a hundred Privy Councillors swore allegiance to him as "our only lawful and rightful Liege Lord, Edward the Eighth, by the Grace of God, of Great Britain, Ireland, and the British Dominions, beyond the Seas, King, Defender of the Faith, Emperor of India . . ."

He addressed the assembled company: "When my father stood here twenty-six years ago, he declared that one of the objects of his life would be to uphold constitutional government. In this I am determined to follow in my father's footsteps and to work as he did throughout his life for the happiness and welfare of all classes of my subjects. I place my reliance upon the loyalty and affection of my peoples throughout the Empire, and upon the wisdom of their Parliaments, to support me in this heavy task, and I pray God will guide me to perform it."

Next morning he came to join a few friends whom he had invited to watch the proclamation of his accession by Garter King of Arms, from the window of a room in St. James's Palace. Mrs. Simpson was among them. On leaving the ceremony she said to him, "This has made me realize how different your life is going to be." The King replied, pressing her arm, "Wallis, there will be a difference. But nothing can ever change my feelings towards you."

King George V lay in state for four days in Westminster Hall, while a million of his people filed past his coffin to pay their last respects—four times as many as had filed past the coffin of his father, King Edward VII. On the new King's suggestion he and his brothers, in full-dress uniform, with swords reversed, did duty one night on guard at the four corners of the catafalque. Five kings marched in his funeral procession to St. George's Chapel at Windsor—only two fewer, despite the constitutional upheavals of the age, than had followed that of King Edward. As the coffin was lowered into the royal vault, with the words, "Earth to earth, ashes to ashes, dust to dust," King Edward VIII scattered it with earth from a silver bowl.

The Tomb of King George V in St. George's Chapel, Windsor.

Chapter
IX

*I*n some ways the King's life changed, now that he had ascended the Throne; in other ways it carried on much as before. More of his time was taken up with the routine business of kingship. He gave continual audiences to Cabinet ministers, ambassadors, bishops, colonial governors, officials, important persons, delegations from public bodies. He was inundated with office work, to which he had never taken kindly, spending hours at a desk where the State papers, to which his father had denied him access, piled up incessantly in their red dispatch-boxes, demanding his attention and signature.

He preferred what he called his "field work," inspecting the armed forces and fulfilling public engagements in various parts of the country. On St. David's Day he delivered his first official broadcast as King, adding a paragraph of his own to the draft put before him:

> "I am better known to you as Prince of Wales— as a man who, during the war and since, has had the opportunity of getting to know the people of every country of the world, under all conditions and circumstances. And, although I now speak to you as King, I am still that same man who has had that experience and whose constant effort it will be to continue to promote the well-being of his fellow men."

As befitted one who had not grown up, as his father had done, in the reign and beneath the aura of Queen Victoria, it had always been his intention to modernize the monarchy in such ways as were still compatible with its traditional glory and strength. He would be the first true twentieth-century monarch,

King Edward VIII in the uniform of the Seaforth Highlanders.

ABOVE AND OPPOSITE: The White Drawing Room in Buckingham Palace.

breaking down some of the more rigid conventions of a court which he saw as "at least sexagenarian in composition and outlook," cutting red-tape and reducing formality wherever he could, refusing to be a prisoner of the past and, as King Edward VIII, leading a life freer and more flexible and more in tune with the times than King George V had done.

His first actions on his accession set this trend. He abolished the "Sandringham time" of his father, by which the clocks, in the interests of royal punctuality, were kept half an hour fast. His first journey as King was made by air. He abolished the frock-coat for wear at Court. He drove a station wagon. He moved into Buckingham Palace but "felt lost in its regal immensity" and preferred to do much of his work at The Fort. He modernized Sandringham and Balmoral and drastically cut down their running expenses. He appeared, and was photographed in the street, on a rainy London day, walking a few steps from the Palace to the offices of the Duchy of Cornwall, with an umbrella over his head. This delighted most of his subjects but dismayed those in authority and provoked the comment from one: "The monarchy must remain aloof and above the commonplace. We can't have the King doing this kind of thing. He has the Daimler."

Throughout his life King George had adhered, with scrupulous precision, to a time-table of social engagements which included his presence with a party on the moors of Balmoral for the opening of the grouse-shooting season on August 12. But King Edward, as Prince of Wales, had formed the habit of going abroad every summer, usually to sun himself on the beaches of the Mediterranean, and saw no reason to change his ways now that he had ascended the Throne. Thus early in August 1936 he chartered for his holiday a large yacht, the *Nahlin,* and set off for a cruise down the Dalmatian coast of the Adriatic and into the Aegean. As in previous years, an honoured guest on board was Mrs. Simpson. Her husband did not accompany her.

The ultimate objective of the cruise was an unofficial visit, of some political import, to Istanbul. The British Government had signed a satisfactory agreement on the future security of the Straits with Kemal Atatürk, the ruler of Turkey, and the King's visit was intended as a gesture of goodwill to the Turks, with

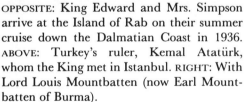

OPPOSITE: King Edward and Mrs. Simpson arrive at the Island of Rab on their summer cruise down the Dalmatian Coast in 1936. ABOVE: Turkey's ruler, Kemal Atatürk, whom the King met in Istanbul. RIGHT: With Lord Louis Mountbatten (now Earl Mountbatten of Burma).

whom the Government was now negotiating on matters of commerce and finance. It was the first visit in history of a British sovereign to Turkey—and it was a resounding success.

On the King's part, it was a highly creditable exercise in personal diplomacy, worthy to rank with those foreign excursions of his grandfather, King Edward VII, which contributed to the *Entente Cordiale* between Britain and France. In a number of informal talks, such as suited them both, the King and Atatürk soon established cordial relations, which helped to create a new climate of Turkish public feeling towards Britain. For many years to come, a bright-coloured picture of the two rulers, side by side beneath their respective national flags, was to adorn coffee-house walls throughout the country, as the happy symbol of a new Anglo-Turkish *Entente Cordiale*.

Atatürk's special train took the King and his party to Sofia, in Bulgaria, King Boris himself driving the engine for the last part of its journey. Passing through Yugoslavia they reached Vienna, whose romantic atmosphere the King

Balmoral Castle was built for Queen Victoria and the Prince Consort. In 1936 Mrs. Simpson visited the castle as a guest of the King during two weeks of grouse-shooting.

OPPOSITE: Edward VIII in parliamentary robes. He was now forty-two.

and Wallis Simpson had enjoyed together before. The King then did a fortnight's duty on the grouse-moors of Balmoral, where Mrs. Simpson, as recorded in the Court Circular, was one of his house-party. At the beginning of October he returned to London, to face a major crisis in his personal life and that of the monarchy.

Two months earlier Mrs. Simpson had filed a petition for divorce against her husband, from whom she had separated, and the case was to be heard in a few weeks' time. Earlier in the summer the King had invited them both to a dinner at York House to meet Mr. Baldwin. "It's got to be done," he had said to her with a smile. "Sooner or later my Prime Minister must meet my future wife." Mrs. Simpson was startled. She had long known that he was cherishing in his mind the dream of marrying her. But this was the first time he had put any such proposal into words.

It was clear to her that the time had come for the King to marry. *The Times,* on his accession, had expressed concern at the fact that in his new and

194

The King leaves Hyde Park through
Wellington Arch at the head of his
Guards after the presentation of new
colors. During the procession back to the
Palace a scene was created as a man in
the crowd threw a loaded revolver at the
King, but it hit the pavement close to
the King's horse. RIGHT: In the Palace
courtyard.

Driving in state to hold the third levee of his reign. OPPOSITE: He accompanies his brothers to the Trooping of the Colour.

arduous duties he would "lack the help and counsel of a consort." Mrs. Simpson had realized that he might well decide to settle down with an acceptable bride. "I was prepared," she afterwards wrote, "to take whatever hurt was in store for me, when the day of reckoning came." When he now talked of marrying her, she exclaimed, "David, you mustn't talk this way. The idea is impossible. They'd never let you!" "I'm well aware of all that," was his light-hearted reply. "But rest assured, I will manage it somehow."

At the dinner, Mrs. Simpson found the Baldwins "pleasant but distant." The next time she dined at York House, she came, as the Court Circular recorded, without her husband. These successive announcements attracted the notice of the American press. *Time* magazine, after the first, referred to Mrs. Simpson as "known to the world press as King Edward's favourite dancing partner, his companion on numerous holiday excursions." After the second, they quoted insurance rates at Lloyd's against the King's marriage as shortening from 11-1 to 5-1. But the British press kept silent; the general public remained ignorant of the affair. Those in authority, though the impending divorce was no secret and gossip was prevalent, did nothing throughout the long summer. Mr.

Baldwin, for the sake of his health, took a two-month rest from all official duties.

On his return to Downing Street Mr. Baldwin was confronted, as he put it later, "with a vast volume of correspondence," from "British subjects and American citizens of British origin in the United States of America, from some of the Dominions and from this country, all expressing perturbation and uneasiness at what was then appearing in the American press." In the middle of October, with the hearing of the divorce case barely a fortnight ahead, he reached the conclusion, as he later told Parliament, "that it was essential that somebody should see His Majesty and warn him of the difficult situation that might arise later if occasion was given for a continuation of this kind of gossip and of criticism, and the danger that might come if that gossip and that criticism spread from the other side of the Atlantic to this country." He thus asked the King for an audience in the privacy of The Fort.

Speaking, as he assured his Sovereign, not merely as his Premier and Counsellor but as a friend, he referred to the prevalent rumours and confessed to two anxieties—their effect on public opinion in the Dominions and at home; their effect on the position of the monarchy. The importance of the integrity of the Crown was "far greater than it had ever been, being as it is not only the last link of the Empire that is left, but the guarantee in this country . . . against many evils that have affected and afflicted other countries. But while this feeling largely depends on the respect that has grown up in the last three generations for the monarchy, it might not take so long, in face of the kind of criticism to which it was being exposed, to lose that power far more rapidly than it was built up, and once lost, I doubt if anything could restore it."

The Prime Minister then pointed out the danger of the divorce proceedings, which under English law would involve a six months' delay before a decree absolute could follow a decree *nisi*. "That period of suspense might be dangerous because then everyone would be talking, and when once the press began . . . a most difficult situation would arise for me, for him, and there might well be a danger which both he and I had seen through all this . . . that there might be sides taken and factions grow up in this country in a matter when no faction ought ever to exist." Finally Mr. Baldwin bluntly asked the King, "Must the case really go on?"

"Mr. Baldwin," he replied, trying to master his feelings, "I have no right to interfere with the affairs of an individual. It would be wrong were I to attempt to influence Mrs. Simpson just because she happens to be a friend of the King's." The interview ended without any question by the Prime Minister as to whether he intended to marry her, once she were free.

Inspecting the Yeomen of the Guard at the Tower of London.

OVERLEAF: The Tower, originally built in the eleventh century by William the Conqueror.

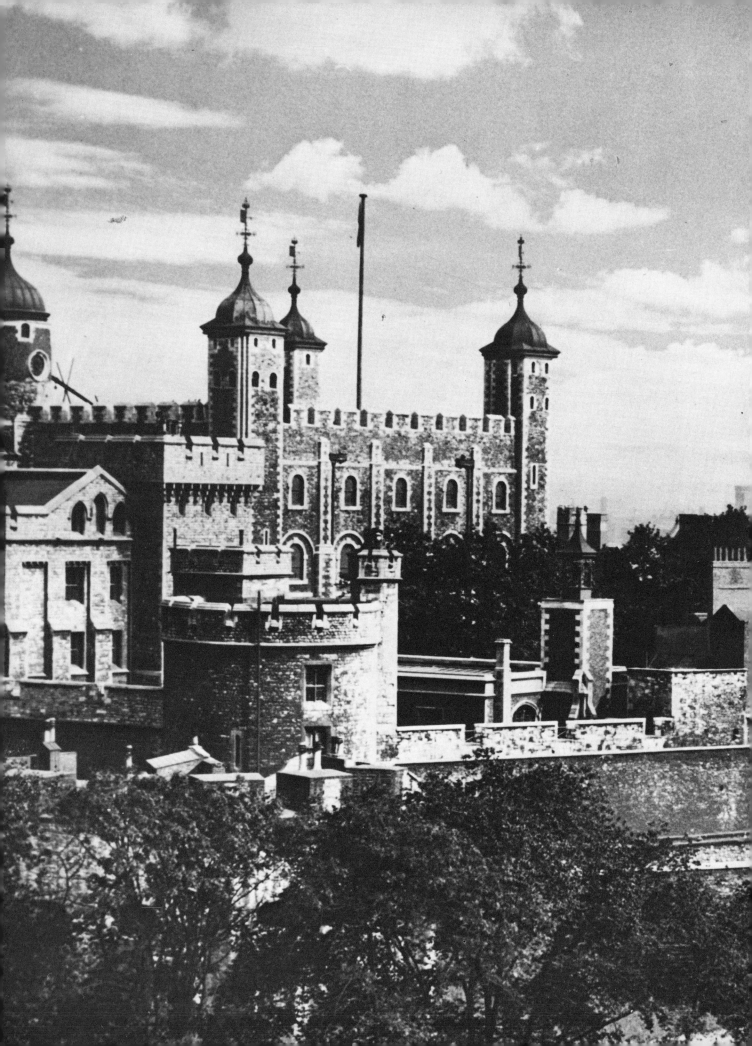

LEFT: In the royal coach. OPPOSITE: After his opening speech from the throne, a cloak of crimson velvet is placed over the King's naval uniform before he leaves the House of Lords, November 3, 1936.

On October 27 Mrs. Simpson was granted a decree *nisi* of divorce, at Ipswich Assizes. Previously the King had asked Lord Beaverbrook, the newspaper proprietor, for his help in preventing the publication of advance news of the case and in having it reported in a straightforward and unsensational manner. With the co-operation of Mr. Esmond Harmsworth, Chairman of the Newspaper Proprietors' Association, and other influential proprietors, a "gentleman's agreement" was reached to this effect and its terms strictly honoured.

On November 3 the King, for the first and last time in his reign, opened Parliament, in state, according to the time-honoured ritual, and read his speech from the Throne. On November 11 he laid a wreath on the Cenotaph in Whitehall in connection with the Armistice Day celebrations. This, as events turned out, was to be the King's last ceremonial duty. For a constitutional crisis of major proportions was imminent.

On November 13, at The Fort, the King, returning from a visit to the Fleet, found awaiting him an urgent and confidential letter from his Private Secretary, Major Alexander Hardinge, which he assumed to have been inspired by Mr. Baldwin. It informed the King that the silence of the British press on his relationship with Mrs. Simpson would not be maintained for more than a few days longer. That day senior members of the Government would meet to discuss the serious situation that was developing. The Government might resign, in which case the King, as Major Hardinge had reason to know, would find nobody able to form a new Government with Parliamentary support. The alternative would be a dissolution of Parliament and a General Election, largely on the issue of the King's personal affairs. This could only cause damage to the Crown—"the corner-stone on which the whole Empire rests." The letter concluded:

> If Your Majesty will permit me to say so, there
> is only one step which holds out any prospect of avoid-

BELOW AND OPPOSITE: On a two-day tour of the distressed areas of South Wales. The King inspects a cooperative farm, accompanied by the Minister of Labour, Ernest Brown.

ing this dangerous situation, and that is for Mrs. Simpson to go abroad *without further delay,* and I would *beg* Your Majesty to give this proposal your earnest consideration before the position has become inevitable. Owing to the changing attitude of the Press, the matter has become one of great urgency.

The King was stunned, not merely by the nature of this bombshell but by the blunt manner in which it was exploded upon him. This, as he saw it, was an ultimatum, a pistol pointed at his head to force him, with the threat of his Government's resignation, to give up the woman he loved and to banish her forthwith from his realm. Major Hardinge, though a man of his own generation, had been one of his father's courtiers. He had chosen him as his own private secretary only on the refusal of Sir Godfrey Thomas, his own close friend and for seventeen years his private secretary as Prince of Wales, to accept the post. The choice had proved a fateful one. Seeing that, on this issue, he could no longer work through Major Hardinge, the King chose another old friend, Mr. Walter Monckton, a distinguished K.C., to act as his personal adviser and official channel of communication with Downing Street.

Already, after his first interview with Mr. Baldwin, he had consulted Mr. Monckton on the imminent crisis, confiding in him certain doubts: "I am beginning to wonder whether I really am the kind of king they want. Am I not a bit too independent? As you know, my make-up is very different from that of my father. I believe they would prefer someone more like him. Well, there is my brother Bertie." Now he told him of his intention to demand, at once, a second interview with Mr. Baldwin.

Then he showed Wallis Simpson the Hardinge letter and explained its significance. Mrs. Simpson was appalled. Her immediate reaction was to insist that she leave the country immediately, as the letter had asked. The King answered peremptorily, "You'll do no such thing. I won't have it. This letter is an impertinence."

Summoning up all her powers of persuasion, she begged the King to let her go. But he was adamant. In the tone of a man whose mind was made up, he announced, "I intend to see the Prime Minister tomorrow. I shall tell him that if the Government is opposed to our marriage, as Alec Hardinge says in his letter, then I am prepared to go."

Never before had he given her a hint of any intention to give up the Throne. She burst into tears. "David, it is madness to think, let alone talk, of such a thing." She implored him not to be so impetuous. There must, she suggested, be some other way out.

But he replied: "I don't believe there can be, after this. I cannot leave this challenge hanging in the air another day." In his eyes it was a challenge to the roots of his pride and his chivalry, which only a faint-hearted man would reject.

King Edward VIII took up the gauntlet with resolution and spirit. On November 16 he received his Prime Minister at Buckingham Palace. For the first time the word "marriage" was mentioned between them. Mr. Baldwin explained that the position of the King's wife differed from that of the wife of any ordinary citizen. For, under the Constitution, she was bound to become Queen. But Mrs. Simpson had been married before, and her marriages had been dissolved by divorce. For this reason, neither his Government nor the British public, for whose moral outlook he pretended to speak, would accept her as Queen.

To this the King replied that marriage had become an indispensable condition to his continued existence, whether as King or as man: "I intend to marry Mrs. Simpson as soon as she is free," he announced. If the Government opposed the marriage, he was "prepared to go."

Mr. Baldwin was startled, and commented, "Sir, that is most grievous news, and it is impossible for me to make any comment on it today."

Along the Mall before breakfast.

During the next few days the King broke the news to his family. His mother, who put duty before love and saw the monarchy as a sacred trust, concealed her consternation behind an iron reserve of self-control. She refused his request that she receive Wallis Simpson and judge for herself. A year or so later she wrote to him, at his request, of her feelings at this time:

> It seemed inconceivable to those who had made
> such sacrifices during the war that you, as their King,
> refused a lesser sacrifice. . . . My feelings for you as a
> Mother remain the same, and our being parted and the
> cause of it grieve me beyond words. After all, all my life
> I have put my Country before everything else, and I
> simply cannot change now.

Queen Mary was not a woman who could easily comprehend, in another, the force of an overpowering personal emotion.

The King's brother, the Duke of York, whose fraternal affection for the King and respect for his qualities were combined with a dread of assuming his Crown, was too much taken aback to express his feelings. From then onwards the King saw little or nothing of his family, determined that this was a constitutional issue which he must face by himself.

Meanwhile he fulfilled a long-standing engagement to visit the depressed areas of South Wales, thus persisting as King in his concern for the unemployed which he had so consistently shown as Prince of Wales. Many years before, when he had planned a similar journey to the coal-fields of Northumberland and Durham, Mr. Baldwin had expressed to him a fear that it might be exploited by the Opposition for political motives. He had been reassured to learn that a leading member of the Conservative Party had sponsored it.

Now the King was accompanied by two Conservative ministers. He made a point of meeting the former Commissioner for the Special Areas, whose report, proposing measures to relieve distress, was in the hands of the Government. He assured groups of ruined miners that he was determined to help their industry, and was quoted in the press as saying, "Something must be done." It was a phrase such as he had often used on similar tours before. It was welcomed by the Liberal press. But it was to be falsely exploited by his Conservative enemies to suggest that he was trying to win popular support for his struggle with the Government.

The King returned to London with little hope in his heart that his abdication could now be avoided. But he was determined to explore every alternative before abandoning the struggle. He consulted a personal friend in the Cabinet, Duff Cooper, who had been one of his guests on his holiday cruise in the Eastern Mediterranean. Mr. Cooper advised delay. He pointed out that five months must inevitably elapse before Mrs. Simpson's decree of divorce was made absolute and she became free to marry again. The question of his marriage could remain until then in abeyance. Let him be patient, ignore the general clamour, and postpone any public decision on his marriage until after his Coronation, when it could be considered in a calmer atmosphere. Such was the counsel of a man of the world.

But the King felt unable to accept it. His grounds were religious. At his coronation he would take the Sacrament as Defender of the Faith, swearing an oath to uphold the doctrines of the Church of England, which does not approve of divorce. To go through the ceremony with a secret intention to marry a divorced person would have meant, as he put it, "being crowned with a lie on my lips." The question of his marriage must be settled before his coronation, not after it.

Lord Beaverbrook and Mr. Duff Cooper, friends of the King.

Another alternative was now suggested by Esmond Harmsworth, the newspaper proprietor who, with Lord Beaverbrook, had helped to ensure the discretion of the press. Let the King contract a morganatic marriage—a legal marriage between a male member of a royal house and a woman not of equal birth, for which there were precedents in history. By this means Mrs. Simpson could be married to the King without becoming Queen, taking instead some such title as Duchess of Lancaster. This course would require the consent of the Cabinet and the passage of a bill through Parliament.

Though dubious as to its prospects of success, the King was ready to consider any possible means of surmounting the constitutional obstacles without forcing a political crisis. Thus he summoned the Prime Minister once more to an audience, and put the proposal formally before him for submission to the Cabinet. Mr. Baldwin explained that it would have to be submitted also to the cabinets of the Dominions. The King authorized him to make this submission. Having done so he realized that he had placed his fate in Mr. Baldwin's hands. Constitutionally, it was his own right as King to consult his own Dominions, independently of his Prime Minister. But it was a right which he did not care to exercise, feeling that this was a matter too delicate for the King to handle in person.

Next day Lord Beaverbrook, interrupting a visit to America at the King's request, returned to England and drove straight to The Fort. Here the King told him of all that he had done, reiterating the refrain, "No marriage, no coronation." Lord Beaverbrook deplored his proposal for a morganatic marriage on the grounds that it was certain to be rejected both by the British Cabinet and by those of the Dominions. He urged the King to withdraw it. Let him adopt instead a strategy of delay, to gain time for "the King's case" to be fairly put forward.

But events, in the view of the King, had moved too far and too fast to be halted. He realized moreover that such a strategy, though it might have worked at an earlier stage, did not suit his true nature: "However carefully I walked, it would involve me in a long course of seeming dissimulation for which I had neither the talent nor the appetite."

Thus the Cabinet met. Mr. Baldwin duly dismissed the idea of the morganatic marriage as impracticable and undesirable, and narrowed the choices for his ministers down to two—either the Government's acceptance of Mrs. Simpson as Queen, or the King's abdication if he persisted in marrying her. These alternatives were agreed by the Cabinet with one dissenting voice—that of Duff Cooper. Meanwhile the question was put to the Dominion premiers, in the form of an equally rigid choice—between a morganatic marriage and abdication. Their replies were a foregone conclusion. "Sir," Lord Beaverbrook exclaimed to the King, "you have put your head on the execution block. All that Baldwin has to do now is to swing the axe."

Nonetheless, as he swung it, the King was determined not to be pushed into any irrevocable decision until his case had been heard by his people. At this eleventh hour Lord Beaverbrook launched a determined campaign to rally support for him, wherever it could be found. This was now to be waged in the open. The news of the crisis, of which the British public was still in the dark, could not be withheld from the press for much longer. As it chanced, it was a pillar of the Church, not of the Government, who broke the story. On December 1, the

On Armistice Day, 1936, with his mother and the Duke of York at the Cenotaph in Whitehall.

210

The King walks with Mrs. Simpson in Salzburg.
OPPOSITE: Their story at last makes the headlines.

Bishop of Bradford, Dr. A. W. F. Blunt, in an address on the Coronation Service to his diocesan conference, used these fateful words:

> "The benefit of the King's coronation depends, under God, on two elements—first on the faith, prayer, and self-dedication of the King himself—and on that it would be improper for me to say anything except commend him, and ask you to commend him to God's grace, which he will so abundantly need, as we all need it—for the King is a man like ourselves—if he is to do his duty faithfully. We hope that he is aware of this need. Some of us wish that he gave more positive signs of his awareness."

Here, for the first time, was implied criticism of the King's private life, expressed publicly. It was reported next day in the press; and the storm at last broke upon the country.

Chapter
X

King Edward VIII had been faced, during these weeks, with a deep conflict between human feelings and royal obligations. He had excelled in his career as Prince of Wales largely because he felt and thought and impressed himself on his people not as a creature apart but as an ordinary human being like the rest of them. His popularity had rested on a happy fusion between his private and his public self. But now, in the first year of his reign as King, the two fell apart, irreconcilably.

For the first time in his life he had found, at the age of forty-two, what he had always, consciously or otherwise, been seeking—a woman whom he could love deeply and unselfishly, a human relationship to fill a void in his inner life which had hitherto left him with a sense of incompleteness. But by the tragic irony of his position, he could, in this crisis, keep public affection and respect only by acting against the deepest instincts of his own private nature—by ceasing to be his complete self. Here was a conflict not unfamiliar in the history of royalty, but one which the ordinary human being does not have to face. It called for superhuman qualities; and the King, as he had consistently shown, was but human. As he put it many years later: "The situation developed so suddenly and many of my countrymen saw it out of focus. I'd been built up and up in the public imagination, and then suddenly pulled down during the crisis, and finally revealed as the man I was."

The British press, which had consistently lauded the Prince of Wales for a public life devoted to his country's service, now turned its batteries against him as King, for seeking to reconcile it with a love which answered his innermost needs. "All my life," as the King himself saw it, "I had been the passive clay which it had enthusiastically worked into the hackneyed image of a Prince Charming. Now it had whirled around, and was bent upon demolishing the natural man who

In the uniform of the Scots Guards.

had been there all the time." During the next days, the *Times*, the *Morning Post*, the *Daily Telegraph*, the papers of the Conservative Establishment, thundered sonorously forth on the perils that menaced the nation and the Empire if the King's "private inclination" were allowed to prevail over his "public duty." It was incumbent upon the King as a man to merge himself wholly in his kingly office. The proprietor of the Labour organ, the *Daily Herald*, favoured the King, as did many Opposition Members of Parliament, but was overruled by the party bosses controlling its policy, who favoured his abdication. All those opposing him set their faces against compromise and pressed for a rapid solution.

Nonetheless, the King had his friends and supporters. The Liberal *News Chronicle* came out staunchly on his side, first favouring a morganatic marriage and then, when it had been rejected by Mr. Baldwin and by the Dominion Prime Ministers, pleading for delay: "Neither the people of Britain and the Empire nor their representatives in Parliament have ever had the issue explained to them—much less been given an opportunity of expressing their own opinions upon it. If in these circumstances the King feels himself compelled to abdicate, there is danger of the growth of a feeling of grave resentment. Both Parliament and the people need time for reflection." So spoke the acknowledged keeper of the British "nonconformist conscience." Unexpectedly, similar views were expressed, at the other end of the religious scale, by the *Catholic Times*.

The two popular papers, with the largest circulations, supported the King. Lord Rothermere's *Daily Mail* stressed the view of his subjects that "he is a man as well as a King, and that, being a man, he is not exempt from mortal emotions. They resent most strongly the one-sided attacks which have been made upon him by censorious critics." Lord Beaverbrook's *Daily Express* declared that Mr. Baldwin and his Government "do not reflect the true feelings of the British people if they base their opposition to the marriage—as their press supporters do—on the grounds that Mrs. Simpson has divorced her husband." The desire for divorce was now generally recognized. Had its opponents "to be gratified by the entire Empire giving up a splendid and hard-working King?" Later the paper insisted, "No Government can stand in the King's way if he is resolved to walk that way. . . . Let the King give his decisions to the people and let him give the reasons for them too." But an American columnist, Arthur Brisbane, foretold the outcome. Recalling the bulletin on the night of King George's death, "The King's life is moving peacefully towards its close," he wrote: "It seems to me this night that the reign of his son is moving to its close, although not peacefully."

Lord Beaverbrook had worked hard among his colleagues and friends to achieve a united front among the King's press supporters. But he confessed him-

Big Ben and (left) the House of Commons, in which a storm arose over the King's intended marriage and abdication.

self hampered by the King's own attitude. As he afterwards recorded: "Through-out all the days of public controversy he shackled the Press that was favourable to himself. He would allow us no liberty in expressing our views or in arguing strongly for his cause. . . . As a result, the pro-Baldwin Press had the field all to itself." If the King did this, it was with the highest and most honourable intentions. "In the chaos around me," he recalled, "I had three instinctive desires: to dampen the uproar if I could; to avoid the responsibility of splitting the nation and jeopardising the Monarchy on the issue of my personal happiness; and to protect Wallis from the full blast of sensationalism about to overwhelm us both."

Meanwhile, in another audience, Mr. Baldwin had confirmed to him the refusal of the Dominions to accept a morganatic marriage. The King asked, "What about Parliament?" The answer, Mr. Baldwin was sure, would be the same.

"But Parliament," the King persisted, "has not been consulted. The issue has never been presented."

Mr. Baldwin replied, unruffled: "I have caused inquiries to be set afoot in the usual manner. The response has been such as to convince my colleagues and myself that the people would not approve of Your Majesty's marriage with Mrs. Simpson." It was said of Mr. Baldwin that he was the only man in Britain who knew on Friday what the House of Commons would be thinking on Monday. "I have always believed," he once explained, with a shy smile, "in the week-end. But how they [the M.P.'s] do it I don't know. I suppose they talk to the station-master."

Thus he now summed up for the King the three alternative courses still available to him: to renounce the marriage; to marry contrary to the advice of his ministers; to abdicate. This left the King, as he saw it, with only one choice. "Whether on the Throne or not, Mr. Baldwin, I shall marry; and however painful the prospect, I shall, if necessary, abdicate in order to do so."

But he had not yet altogether given up hope. If he could explain his case to the people both in Britain and in the Dominions direct, he believed that he could clarify confusion, relieve tension, and foster an atmosphere in which reason and justice might prevail. He thus prepared the draft of a broadcast for delivery over the BBC—though he had his doubts as to whether he would be allowed (or in terms of the constitutional formula "advised") by the Government to deliver it. It was an appeal to the hearth and the home, presenting his problem in human rather than in constitutional terms. His listeners, he felt, knew him well enough to realize that he would never enter into a marriage of convenience. He would tell them simply that, after a long time, he had at last found the woman whom he wished to make his wife and that, having found her, he was determined to marry her. His draft continued:

Neither Mrs. Simpson nor I have ever sought to insist that she should be Queen. All we desired was that our married happiness should carry with it a proper title and dignity for her, befitting my wife.

Conceiving the idea that it might be well for him to withdraw briefly from the overheated atmosphere, leaving a Council of State in control, he concluded:

Now that I have at last been able to take you into my confidence, I feel it is best to go away for a while so that you may reflect calmly and quietly, but without undue delay, on what I have said. Nothing is dearer to my heart than that I should return; but whatever may befall, I shall always have a deep affection for my country, for the Empire, and for you all.

The King broadcasts his Accession message at the B.B.C. on St. David's Day, March 1, 1936.

The broadcast was read and approved, with a few suggested changes of phrase, by Winston Churchill, though he, too, doubted whether Mr. Baldwin would approve its delivery. Their forebodings proved correct. Interpreting the broadcast as an attempt to appeal to the people over the heads of the Executive, the Cabinet rejected it on constitutional grounds. Thus there vanished the sole legitimate means by which the King, in this crisis of his reign, could appeal to his subjects.

Mr. Churchill, contending that the Executive were illegally forcing a constitutional issue for political reasons, now emerged as the King's lustiest and most eloquent champion. Impressed, at a mass-meeting in the Albert Hall, by the storm of applause and cries of "Long live the King" which greeted a loyal and friendly reference in his speech to the Sovereign, he became convinced that abdication could still be avoided if the country were given time to recover from the shock of the news and consider the situation in a more dispassionate atmosphere. Already he had pleaded in the House of Commons that no irrevocable step should be taken before Parliament expressed its views. To the King—whom he saw with Mr. Baldwin's permission—he said: "Sir, it is a time for reflection. You must allow time for the battalions to march." In a statement to the press, following a letter to the Prime Minister, he wrote:

> I plead for time and patience. The nation must
> realize the character of the constitutional issue. There
> is no question of any conflict between the King and
> Parliament. Parliament has not been consulted in any
> way, nor allowed to express any opinion. The question
> is whether the King is to abdicate upon the advice of
> the Ministry of the day. No such advice has ever before
> been tendered to a Sovereign in Parliamentary times.

The matter, he contended, was of no constitutional urgency. The act contemplated by the Sovereign could certainly not be accomplished for another five months, and might conceivably never be accomplished. On such a hypothetical basis, "the supreme sacrifice of abdication and potential exile of the Sovereign" found no support in the British Constitution. No ministry had the authority to advise it, without ascertaining the will of Parliament. This could perhaps be done through messages from the Sovereign to Parliament, and after their due consideration, addresses of reply by both Houses. The King's ministers had no right to put pressure on him by obtaining an assurance from the leader of the Opposition, as the Prime Minister had done, that, if they resigned, he would not form another Government. This was tantamount to an ultimatum. "Why," he inquired, "cannot time be granted?"

Finally Mr. Churchill stressed the human and personal aspect:

> The King has been for many weeks under the
> greatest strain, moral and mental, that can fall upon a
> man. Not only has he been inevitably subjected to the
> extreme stress of his public duty, but also to the agony
> of his own personal feelings. Surely, if he asks for time
> to consider the advice of his Ministers . . . he should not
> be denied.

The churches, he added, stood for charity. Their influence, in the interests of tolerance, should not oppose a period of reflection. The politicians should show "a loyal and Christian patience." He concluded:

> If an abdication were to be hastily extorted the
> outrage so committed would cast its shadow forward
> across many chapters of the history of the British
> Empire.

When the question was next raised in the House of Commons, Mr. Churchill, "who had been leaning forward in his corner seat below the gangway, with set and flushed face," rose again to put his familiar request that "no irrevocable steps should be taken." But this time he was howled down by a hysterical Chamber with cries of "No!" and "Sit down!" This, in the words of the *Times*, was Mr. Churchill's "Bad Day." He had been subjected to "the most striking rebuff of modern Parliamentary history."

To protect Mrs. Simpson from the storm, the King had at last agreed to her suggestion that she go abroad. She left England secretly in the company of his friend, Lord Brownlow. But the French press got wind of her journey, and they were pursued across France by an army of reporters whom they contrived, with some ingenuity, to evade, finally reaching the refuge of the villa, near Cannes, of her American friends, Mr. and Mrs. Herman Rogers.

That evening the King left Buckingham Palace and took up permanent quarters at The Fort, where, besieged though it became by reporters and photographers, he could reach his final decision free from popular pressure and alone with his thoughts. As he drove for the last time out of the gates of the Palace a knot of onlookers cheered him. It was a spontaneous tribute which consoled him by the proof that he was still held in affection.

Signs of this grew during the next days as scattered groups, animated by spontaneous sympathy and perhaps a sense of fair play, gathered here or outside No. 10 Downing Street or toured the city in cars, singing "God Save the

King" and "For He's a Jolly Good Fellow"; shouting "God save the King—from Stanley Baldwin;" chalking STAND BY THE KING on blank walls; parading with placards, HANDS OFF OUR KING: ABDICATION MEANS REVOLUTION. In such ways there germinated a movement which became known in the press as "the King's Party," and which reflected especially the views of the youth of the country.

Among his friends there were those who would have liked the King to exploit this popular sentiment, whether by appealing to the public in person or by allowing them to do so on his behalf. But the King declined to put his popularity to the test for fear of dividing the nation and permanently damaging the Crown. "By making a stand for myself," he afterwards wrote, "I should have left the scars of a civil war. . . . The price of my marriage under such circumstances would have been the infliction of a grievous wound on the social unity of my native land and on that wider unity that is the Empire." Had he won, and thus retained his throne, "the cherished conception of the monarchy above politics would have been shattered and the party system might have suffered a fatal hurt. Could Wallis and I have hoped to find happiness under that condition? . . . The answer was No."

Thus after a sleepless night the King reached his final decision to abdicate.

The crown of England which Edward VIII was never to wear. St. Edward's Crown, copied in the time of Charles II from the ancient one of Edward the Confessor, was worn at the coronations of Charles II, James II, William III, Anne, George I, George II, George III, George V, and was also to be worn by George VI and Elizabeth II.

Chapter

XI

*T*he King's friends, largely inspired by Lord Beaverbrook, were engaged meanwhile on a final manœuvre to avert this decision and save him his throne. If, as was evident, the King would not renounce Mrs. Simpson, then Mrs. Simpson should be encouraged to renounce the King. This, in Lord Beaverbrook's view, need not be a final and irrevocable decision. What he envisaged was a postponement of the question of marriage, designed to relieve the present tension and gain time for reflection. The friend they chose to put this case before her was Lord Brownlow, who as it chanced had been chosen by the King to escort her to France.

She needed little persuasion. An American, unversed in British constitutional matters, she had never imagined that her relationship with the King could lead to his renunciation of the Throne. Always she had been reassured by his injunctions to leave everything to him, his determination to "work things out my own way," his over-optimistic conviction that "there are things I still can do." "Nothing that I had seen," she was to write later, "had made me appreciate how vulnerable the King really was, how little power he could actually command, how little his wishes counted against those of his ministers and Parliament." Nothing that he had said had prepared her for the prospect of his abdication, which she now saw as a step to be prevented at any possible cost.

On her journey across France she telephoned to him, shouting over a bad line in the code which they had devised for security reasons, to beg him not to "step down," to do nothing impulsive, to take the advice of his friends. From Cannes she abandoned the code to plead with him earnestly: "David, please listen to your friends. . . . Nothing will be lost, nothing will be changed by your waiting." Unconvinced by his assurances, she then agreed with Lord Brownlow

Mrs. Simpson in Paris.

225

that if the abdication were to be prevented she must publicly renounce him. Lord Brownlow, to check the King in his course, favoured a strong and unequivocal public statement that she had no thought of marrying him. Mrs. Simpson, from her understanding of the King's nature and her knowledge of his own understanding of hers, feared that so sudden and harsh a declaration might well have the opposite reaction upon him. Thus a statement, in more moderate language, was issued:

> Mrs. Simpson throughout the last few weeks has invariably wished to avoid any action or proposal

Supporters of the King make their sentiments clear by parading in the streets.

which would hurt or damage His Majesty or the Throne. Today her attitude is unchanged, and she is willing, if such action would solve the problem, to withdraw from a situation that has been rendered both unhappy and untenable.

Mrs. Simpson read the statement to the King over the telephone. He sounded to her incredulous, then angry and hurt. Finally he said, "Go ahead if you wish; it won't make any difference."

For a moment the publication of this "act of renunciation" relieved ten-

Stanley Baldwin on his way to a Cabinet meeting.

sion at home. "We can rejoice," Lord Beaverbrook's *Daily Express* declared. "The crisis has passed into history." The Stock Exchange rallied. The House of Commons was distinctly more cheerful. Mr. Baldwin, hoping to clinch the matter by obtaining from Mrs. Simpson a withdrawal of her divorce petition, sent her solicitor, Mr. Theodore Goddard, to Cannes. Over the telephone she was warned by the King of his imminent arrival. "You must not listen to this man," he insisted. "Do not be influenced by anything he says."

Mrs. Simpson assured Mr. Goddard that she would do anything in her power to keep the King on the Throne. Falling in with his proposal, she telephoned to the King and told him that she had agreed to withdraw her divorce petition. He replied that it was too late. He had decided to abdicate immediately and was already in the process of doing so.

Mrs. Simpson decided on one last drastic step. She would leave Europe. She would fly out of his reach, perhaps to friends in China. Sick at heart, she telephoned again to The Fort. But the King cut her short. "It's all over," he said. "The Instrument of Abdication is already prepared. . . . The only conditions on which I can stay here are if I renounce you for all time. And this, of course, I will not do. The Cabinet has met twice today, and I have given them my final word. I will be gone from England within forty-eight hours." In short, Mrs. Simpson could go wherever she chose. But he would follow her to the ends of the earth.

She broke down in tears, bitterly conscious of failure. Mrs. Rogers, her hostess, tried to comfort her: "You have done everything that could be expected of a woman in this situation. No one will blame you." As the King himself saw it later: "She tried throughout to make me turn back, and she would have succeeded had I not loved her so desperately and therefore been so determined."

From the outset the King in his intention, if need be, to abdicate, had been fortified by the belief that his brother the Duke of York, cast as he was in the mould of their father King George V, trained to royal duties as heir presumptive for twenty-six years, and blessed with a wife well-equipped to be Queen, could replace him on the Throne without in any way damaging the prestige of the monarchy. "I was a good Prince of Wales," he said afterwards, "but I don't know whether I should be a good King." That his brother would "make a fine King" he was never for an instant in doubt.

The Duke of York himself, shy in manner and modest in character, was tormented by doubts as to his own fitness for so heavy a task. Throughout the

At Aldershot, with his brother George.

228

crisis he endured agonies of suspense. "If the worst happens and I have to take over," he wrote to one of the King's private secretaries, "you can be assured that I will do my best to clear up the inevitable mess, if the whole fabric does not crumble under the shock and strain of it all." To another he wrote: "I feel like the proverbial 'sheep being led to the slaughter.'"

Day after day passed when his brother, determined to settle the matter in his own way, refused to see him, and he remained uncertain of his fate. Finally, one evening, the King sent for him, and "the awful and ghastly suspense of waiting was over. I found him pacing up and down the room and he told me his decision that he would go." Going home to dinner, the Duke returned to The Fort later in the evening. "I felt once having got there I was not going to leave. As he is my eldest brother I had to be there to try and help him in his hour of need."

The next evening he dined at The Fort. Mr. Baldwin was among the guests. So was the Duke of Kent; this was the first time for many days that the King had opened the doors of his house to his family. The King, rising to the occasion, became, as his brother recalled it, "the life and soul of the party, telling the Prime Minister things I am sure he had never heard before about unemployed centres etc. (referring to his visit in S. Wales). I whispered to W. M. '& this is the man we are going to lose.' One couldn't, nobody could believe it."

The King made one last request of Mr. Baldwin—that simultaneously with the Abdication Bill he should submit to Parliament a second "divorce bill," making Mrs. Simpson's divorce absolute forthwith, so that he could join her abroad and their marriage could take place immediately. This measure had been proposed by Mr. Walter Monckton, "to lift the ordeal of a prolonged separation from two human beings who had already been through the fire." The King had acceded to Mr. Baldwin's insistence on speed in reaching his final decision. This would give him the chance to show reciprocal respect to the King's own wish for it in the matter of his personal needs. Mr. Baldwin acceded to his request as a just one, adding, to the King's surprise, the rash promise that he would resign if the Cabinet rejected it. But the Cabinet, bowing to the churchmen among its ministers, did reject it. And Mr. Baldwin did not resign.

For the King, all was now over. On the morning of December 10, 1936, he signed at The Fort a message to Parliament embodying his Instrument of Abdication. It ran:

> After long and anxious consideration, I have determined to renounce the Throne to which I succeeded on the death of my Father, and I am now communicating this my final and irrevocable decision. Realising as

I do the gravity of this step, I can only hope that I shall have the understanding of my people in the decision I have taken and the reasons which have led me to take it.

I will not enter now into my private feelings, but I would beg that it should be remembered that the burden which constantly rests upon the shoulders of a Sovereign is so heavy that it can only be borne in circumstances different from those in which I now find myself.

I conceive that I am not overlooking the duty that rests on me to place in the forefront the public interest when I declare that I am conscious that I can no longer discharge this heavy task with efficiency, or with satisfaction to myself.

The terms of the Instrument followed:

I, Edward the Eighth, of Great Britain, Ireland, and the British Dominions beyond the seas, Emperor of India, do hereby declare My irrevocable determination to renounce the Throne for Myself and for My descendants, and My desire that effect be given to this Instrument of Abdication immediately.

To this the King added that he deeply appreciated "the spirit which has actuated the appeals which have been made to me to take a different decision, and I have, before reaching my final determination, most fully pondered over them. But my mind is made up. Moreover, further delay cannot but be most injurious to the people whom I have tried to serve as Prince of Wales and as King. . . . I take my leave of them in the confident hope that the course which I have thought it right to follow is that which is best for the stability of the Throne and Empire and the happiness of my peoples. . . . I am most anxious that there should be no delay of any kind in giving effect to the Instrument which I have executed, and that all necessary steps should be taken immediately to secure that the lawful successor, my brother His Royal Highness the Duke of York, should ascend the Throne."

The document was signed "Edward, R. I.," and witnessed by his three brothers, who signed in turn. It was then taken to London for its presentation to Parliament that afternoon, and passage into law for his own Royal Assent next morning. The Prime Minister, who was to present it, asked the King for any points he might like to mention in his speech to the House. He mentioned two: a reference to the Duke of York, his affection for him as a brother and his confidence that he deserved and would receive the whole Empire's support; a reference to "the other person most intimately concerned," and an acknowledgement of her efforts to dissuade him from the decision he had taken. Mr. Baldwin mentioned the first point, but omitted the second—unlike the King who, in his own abdication broadcast, deferred to Mr. Baldwin's request to mention his own considerate attitude.

In the speech, to a tense and emotional House—"a theatre," as he put it, "which is being watched by the whole world"—the Prime Minister avoided fine phrases of rhetoric. He judged it best to narrate with a studied simplicity, but with no less dramatic effect, his version of the day-to-day events of the past two months, from his first interview with the King until today's abdication. He carefully refrained from overt comment or criticism, praise or blame, leaving his audience to interpret his words as they chose. But he had the grace to commend the King's dignity "in this hour of his trial." He referred also to the strain which the crisis had placed upon himself. He concluded with a peroration on Parliament and the Crown as the guardians of democracy and freedom.

In the speeches which followed, Mr. Maxton, a firebrand of the Left, spoke with human sympathy for the King, and wished him future happiness. Two alternatives had faced him: "to continue lonely, disappointed, bitter, ruling the Empire, or else do what he has done, to throw up royalty and remain a man. We shall all commend him for that choice of the two." His noblest valediction, both as a king and as a man, was spoken by Mr. Churchill:

> "No Sovereign has ever conformed more strictly or more faithfully to the letter of the Constitution than his present Majesty. In fact, he has voluntarily made a sacrifice for the peace and strength of his realm, which goes far beyond the bounds required by the Law and Constitution. . . . In this Prince there were discerned qualities of courage, of simplicity, of sympathy, and, above all, of sincerity, qualities rare and precious which might have made his reign glorious in the annals of this ancient monarchy. It is the acme of tragedy that these very virtues should, in the private sphere, have led only to this melancholy and bitter conclusion. But although today our hopes are withered, still I will assert that his personality will not go down uncherished to future ages, that it will be particularly remembered in the homes of his poorer subjects, and that they will ever

Mounted police clearing crowds from Parliament Square.

wish from the bottoms of their hearts for his private
peace and happiness, and for the happiness of those
who are dear to him.''

Next day, his last on the Throne, the King invited Mr. Churchill to luncheon at The Fort, to bid him good-bye and to ask from him ''the final brush-
strokes'' to a farewell broadcast which he had drafted for delivery to the people
of Britain that evening. While they sat at table, he ceased to be King and
became once more, as he had been at his birth, Prince Edward. There were
tears in Mr. Churchill's eyes as he bade him farewell at the door. Tapping out
a measure with his stick, he recited lines from the historic ode by Andrew
Marvell on the beheading of Charles I:

> ''He nothing common did or mean
> Upon that memorable scene.''

Before making his broadcast Prince Edward dined with his family at Royal Lodge, the home of his brother. Already he had told the news to his mother, whose heart had gone out to her son at the end of their talk, with the words, "And to me, the worst thing is that you won't be able to see her for so long." When the Duke of York joined her afterwards, he "broke down and sobbed like a child." Now, after dinner, Prince Edward drove over to Windsor Castle. Here, in a room overlooking the Great Park and the surrounding English landscape, now blanketed in fog, which he knew and loved so well, he spoke for the last time to the people of Britain:

"At long last I am able to say a few words of my own.

"I have never wanted to withhold anything, but until now it has been not constitutionally possible for me to speak.

"A few hours ago I discharged my last duty as King and Emperor, and now that I have been succeeded by my brother, the Duke of York, my first words must be to declare my allegiance to him. This I do with all my heart.

"You all know the reasons which have impelled me to renounce the Throne. But I want you to understand that in making up my mind I did not forget the country or the Empire which as Prince of Wales, and lately as King, I have for twenty-five years tried to serve. But you must believe me when I tell you that I have found it impossible to carry the heavy burden of responsibility and to discharge my duties as King as I would wish to do without the help and support of the woman I love.

"And I want you to know that the decision I have made has been mine and mine alone. This was a thing I had to judge entirely for myself. The other person most nearly concerned has tried up to the last to persuade me to take a different course. I have made this, the most serious decision of my life, upon a single thought of what would in the end be best for all.

"This decision has been made less difficult to me by the sure knowledge that my brother, with his long training in the public affairs of this country and with his fine qualities, will be able to take my place forthwith, without interruption to the life and progress of the Empire. And he has one matchless blessing, enjoyed by so many of you and not bestowed on me—a happy home with his wife and children.

"During these hard days I have been comforted by my mother and by my family. The Ministers of the Crown, and in particular Mr. Baldwin, the Prime Minister, have always treated me with full consideration. There has never been any constitutional difference between me and them and between me and Parliament. Bred in the constitutional tradition by my father, I should never have allowed any such issue to arise.

"Ever since I was Prince of Wales, and later on when I occupied the Throne, I have been treated with the greatest kindness by all classes, wherever I have lived or journeyed throughout the Empire. For that I am very grateful.

"I now quit altogether public affairs, and I lay down my burden. It may be some time before I return to my native land, but I shall always follow the fortunes of the British race and Empire with profound interest, and if at any time in the future I can be found of service to His Majesty in a private station, I shall not fail.

"And now we all have a new King. I wish him, and you, his people, happiness and prosperity with all my heart. God bless you all. God save the King."

The "woman he loved" listened to the broadcast in the villa at Cannes, lying on the sofa with her hands over her eyes, trying to hide her tears. When it was finished and the others tactfully left her alone, she lay there a long time before she could control herself enough to walk through the house and go upstairs to her room.

The Royal Family listened to the broadcast at Royal Lodge, where the Prince afterwards rejoined them. Then, in the words of Queen Mary, "came the dreadful good-bye, as he was leaving that evening for Austria. The whole thing was too pathetic for words." His brothers stayed until midnight. When they left it was the Prince who, as a subject, bowed to his brother the King. At this Prince George shook his head and cried almost fiercely, "It isn't possible! It isn't happening!"

INSTRUMENT OF ABDICATION

I, Edward the Eighth, of Great Britain, Ireland, and the British Dominions beyond the Seas, King, Emperor of India, do hereby declare My irrevocable determination to renounce the Throne for Myself and for My descendants, and My desire that effect should be given to this Instrument of Abdication immediately.

In token whereof I have hereunto set My hand this tenth day of December, nineteen hundred and thirty six, in the presence of the witnesses whose signatures are subscribed.

SIGNED AT
FORT BELVEDERE
IN THE PRESENCE
OF

OPPOSITE: The Instrument of Abdication, signed by the King, as presented to Parliament. RIGHT: The Archbishop of Canterbury, who broadcast to the nation after the ex-King left for Vienna.

With Walter Monckton the Prince drove in the darkness to Portsmouth. Here he boarded a destroyer, H.M.S. *Fury*, which, unescorted, was to take him across the Channel. Watching the shores of England recede, he reflected how hard it was to give up, not just the Throne, but his country. But of one thing he was certain: "Love had triumphed over the exigencies of politics."

Thus ended the public life of Prince Edward. Now he looked ahead to a life wholly private, in "the world which by my own free will I had chosen." And in the company of the woman with whom he had chosen to share it.

On the Sunday following his departure the Archbishop of Canterbury, whose underlying influence had been implicit throughout the crisis, delivered a broadcast to the nation. In this he uttered words of condemnation which seemed, in the ears of a large congregation of his listeners, to fall sadly short of those precepts of Christian charity to which his Church aspired. Referring to

237

Arrival in Vienna.

the ex-King's "craving," as he chose to put it, for private happiness, the Archbishop continued:

> "Strange and sad it must be that for such a motive, however strongly it pressed upon his heart, he should have disappointed hopes so high, and abandoned a trust so great. Even more strange and sad it is that he should have sought his happiness in a manner inconsistent with the Christian principles of marriage, and within a social circle whose standards and ways of life are alien to all the best instincts and traditions of his people. Let those who belong to this circle know that today they stand rebuked by the judgment of the nation which had loved King Edward. I have shrunk from saying these words. But I have felt compelled for the sake of sincerity and truth to say them.
>
> "Yet for one who has known him since his childhood, who has felt his charm and admired his gifts, these words cannot be the last. How can we forget the high hopes and promise of his youth; his most genuine care for the poor, the suffering, the unemployed; his years of eager service both at home and beyond the seas? It is the remembrance of these things that wrings from our heart the cry—'the pity of it, O, the pity of it.' "

No such unctuous sentiments inspired the Christmas telegram, a week or so later, which reached the Prince in his exile from David Lloyd George, the statesman who had in a sense launched him on his career, first at his investiture

238

at Caernarvon and later as an Ambassador of Empire. Sent from Jamaica, a place mercifully free from the hysteria which had prevailed throughout those weeks in Britain, it read:

BEST CHRISTMAS GREETINGS FROM AN OLD MINISTER OF THE CROWN WHO HOLDS YOU IN HIGH ESTEEM AS EVER AND REGARDS YOU WITH DEEPER LOYAL AFFECTION, DEPLORES THE SHABBY AND STUPID TREATMENT ACCORDED TO YOU, RESENTS THE MEAN AND UNGENEROUS ATTACKS UPON YOU, AND REGRETS THE LOSS SUSTAINED BY THE BRITISH EMPIRE OF A MONARCH WHO SYMPATHISED WITH THE LOWLIEST OF HIS SUBJECTS.

Winston Churchill (in the uniform of an Elder Brother of Trinity House) with Liberal leader Sir Herbert Samuel, at the Accession Council on December 11, 1936.

Chapter

XII

$\mathcal{T}$he Duke of York was proclaimed King George VI. His first step on his accession was to confer upon his brother the title of Duke of Windsor. The new Royal Duke and Mrs. Simpson could not meet until her decree of divorce was made absolute in five months' time. They lived meanwhile, as she put it, in "separate islands of exile," she in France, he in Austria, first with Baron and Baroness Eugène de Rothschild at Schloss Enzesfeld, then at the British Embassy in Vienna. Early in May 1937 they were reunited, at the Château de Candé, near Tours, which had been lent to them for their marriage by a French industrialist, Charles Bedaux.

Here, on May 12, they listened in solemn silence to the broadcast of his brother's coronation service in Westminster Abbey—which might have been his own. Afterwards, the Duke said to the Duchess: "You must have no regrets —I have none. This much I know: what I know of happiness is forever associated with you." On June 3, the anniversary of the birth of King George V, with a small circle of chosen friends around them, they were married in the drawing-room of the Château de Candé. To the Duke's disappointment, no member of his family attended the ceremony. At first no parson of the Church of England would marry them. But finally the Reverend R. Anderson Jardine, a parish vicar in the diocese of Durham, came forward voluntarily, in defiance of his bishop, to do so.

The Duke was officially granted by his brother the "title, style, or attribute" of His Royal Highness. But it was specifically denied to his wife, who became simply the Duchess of Windsor. Thus, in effect, after all, their marriage was "morganatic," though it no longer needed to be so. The Duchess was relegated to a different status from that of the wives of her husband's brothers, their Royal Highnesses the Duchess of York (as she had been) and the Duchess of Gloucester. Neither was of royal blood, but both were raised to royal rank, as the Duchess of Windsor was not.

King George VI is crowned in Westminster Abbey, May 12, 1937.

ABOVE AND BELOW RIGHT: The Coronation procession. The royal coach in front of Buckingham Palace, and mounted troops riding through Admiralty Arch into Trafalgar Square. ABOVE RIGHT: King George VI and Queen Elizabeth with Queen Mary, Princess Elizabeth, Princess Margaret, and other members of the royal party on the balcony at Buckingham Palace following the ceremony at Westminster Abbey.

OVERLEAF: A view of Windsor Castle. In 1917 George V abandoned all German titles for himself and his family, and the royal house became known as the House of Windsor instead of the house of Saxe-Coburg-Gotha. The title "Duke of Windsor," bestowed on the ex-King by his brother King George VI, perpetuates the family name and the name of the castle founded by William the Conqueror near the ancient village on the Thames variously known as Wynde-shour, Wyndsore, and Windelsore.

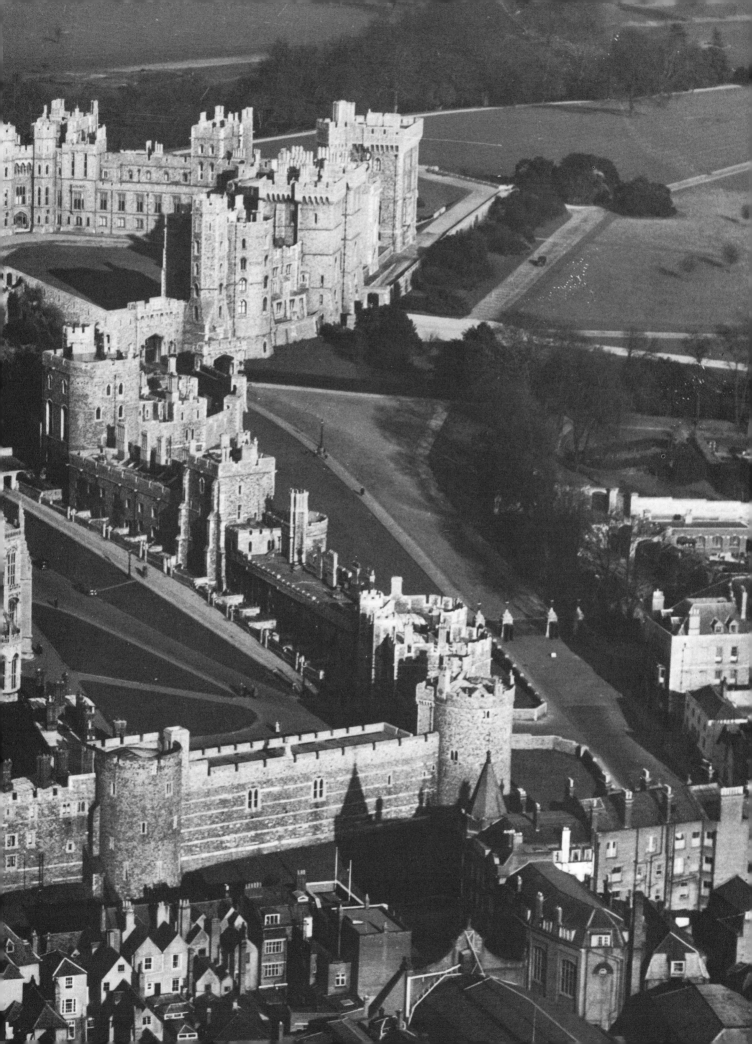

ABOVE: Mrs. Simpson in the garden at the Château de Candé. RIGHT: Decorating the *Mairie* or Town Hall in preparation for the wedding. OPPOSITE: The bride and groom on the balcony at the Château de Candé on their wedding day, June 3, 1937.

246

On honeymoon in Venice.

The Duke and Duchess lived for the present in France, first at Versailles, then alternately at the Villa La Cröe, at Antibes and in a house in Paris which they leased in the Boulevard Suchet near the Bois de Boulogne. "I can see," remarked the Duke with a smile, "that it's going to be the city for us, after all." But he still hoped to return to England, and voiced this wish to Mr. Chamberlain, Mr. Baldwin's successor, on a visit to Paris. The new Prime Minister promised to raise the matter with his Government and, if necessary, the Palace, and to advise him accordingly. But no advice was forthcoming, and the Duke permitted himself the sardonic reflection, "I'm afraid we'll be too old to cross the Channel before my brother and the P.M. stop batting the ball back and forth."

In fact they were to cross it all too soon. For the clouds of war were gathering once more over Europe, as they had done in his youth. As he put it, "This is beginning to smell like 1914 all over again." In the summer of 1939 he broadcast a plea for peace from a commemorative ceremony in Verdun:

> "As I talk to you from this historic place, I am deeply conscious of the presence of the great company of the dead, and I am convinced that could they make their voices heard they would be with me in what I am about to say. For two-and-a-half years I have deliberately kept outside of public affairs and I still propose to do so. I speak for no one but myself and without the previous knowledge of any Government. I speak simply as a soldier of the last war, whose most earnest prayer it is that such cruel and destructive madness shall never again overtake mankind. I break my self-imposed silence now only because of the manifest danger that we may all be drawing nearer to the repetition of the grim events which happened a quarter of a century ago. The grave anxieties of the time in which we live compel me to raise my voice in expression of the universal longing to be delivered from the fears that beset us, and to return to normal conditions."

Those fears were realized a few months later, when Britain declared war upon Germany. The Duke thought only of how to serve his country, in any way his brother thought suitable. He was offered the choice of two jobs—as a member of the British Military Mission at the French General Headquarters outside Paris, or at home, as Regional Commissioner for Civil Defence in Wales. He preferred the prospect of the second. Winston Churchill, now First Lord of the Admiralty, sent a destroyer to Cherbourg, under the command of his cousin, Lord Louis Mountbatten, the King's Naval A.D.C., to escort the Duke and the Duchess across the Channel.

After Prime Minister Chamberlain's vain efforts to appease Hitler, England declared war on Germany on September 3, 1939.

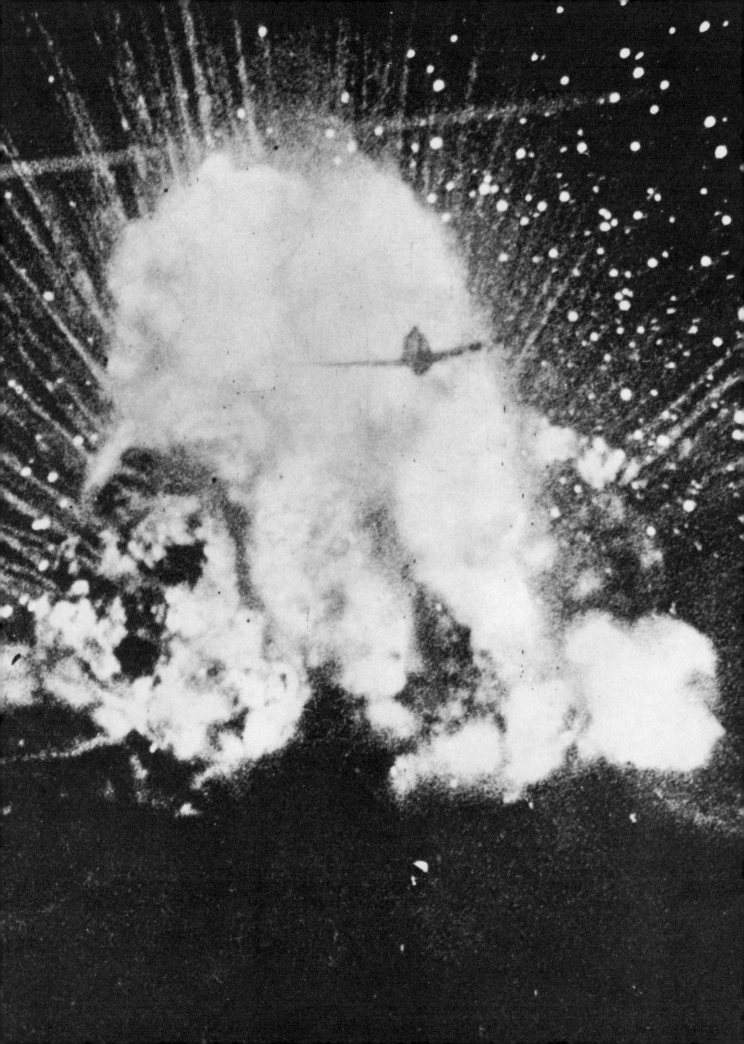

RIGHT AND OPPOSITE: The Duke and Duchess in uniform. The Duke served as major-general with the British Military Mission and the Duchess became a member of the French Red Cross, making frequent trips to hospitals.

King George VI on the Maginot Line.

On a tour of inspection at the front.

OVERLEAF: Air warfare over France.

After the fall of France in 1940, the Duke and Duchess crossed the frontier into Spain. Here they are arriving at the Ritz Hotel in Madrid.

At Portsmouth, where he had embarked for France nearly three years earlier, the Duke was received with royal honours, stepping down the gangway in the darkness onto a red carpet, while a Naval Guard of Honour snapped to attention. Moved by this reception, he remarked afterwards, "I have seen hundreds of guards of honour, but I don't think I was ever prouder of inspecting one." He drove up to London to visit his brother, who agreed with him in his choice of the Regional Commissioner's job.

But after a lapse of some days it was, without explanation, the other job that materialized, and he returned with the Duchess, once again in a destroyer, to France. Here, cheerfully accepting a reduction in rank to major-general, he settled down at G.H.Q. to a staff post with the Military Mission. "War should bring families together, even a royal family," he had said to the Duchess on entering Britain. But to his chagrin, throughout their stay at home no member of his family, or of the Court, had made a sign of recognition that his wife existed.

With the collapse of France in 1940 the Duke and Duchess of Windsor contrived, after a hazardous journey, to cross the frontier into Spain. Reaching Madrid, he was informed in a message from Winston Churchill, now Prime Minister, that two flying boats were to be sent to Lisbon, to fly them home. But before returning the Duke was determined to know two things—what kind of job was in store for him, and whether his wife would now be treated on terms of equality with the wives of his brothers. In a long interchange of telegrams with Winston Churchill he pressed, as a condition of his return, that the Duchess should be received, if only once, by the King and the Queen.

Such recognition at this critical moment seemed to the Duchess herself a matter of minor importance. It could be raised, so she argued, later on. But the Duke's pride was stung and he would not accept her advice. As he said to her: "I won't have them push us into a bottom drawer. It must be the two of us together—man and wife with the same position. . . . Some people will probably say that, with a war on, these trifles should be forgotten. But they are not trifles to me. Whatever I am to be I must be with you; any position I am called upon to fill I can only fill with you."

Winston Churchill tried to reach a compromise with the Palace, but failed. Instead he offered the Duke a post abroad, as Governor of the Bahamas, and this he accepted. Thus the Duke and the Duchess sailed from Lisbon in an American ship, for Nassau. Here they spent the rest of the war, unhappy to be stranded so far from the centre of action, but occupying themselves usefully with such tasks as welfare work for the natives of the islands, the administration of a Red Cross service for shipwrecked victims of the U-boat war, the construction of an air base, and the provision of recreations for its servicemen.

The Duke accepted the post offered him through Winston Churchill as Governor of the Bahamas. ABOVE: The Duke and Duchess of Windsor as they first arrived in Nassau, August 1940.
OPPOSITE AND OVERLEAF: At Government House, Nassau.

The Duke continued his job in the Bahamas for five years. Between his duties he and the Duchess made trips to the United States and Canada. ABOVE: In Canada at the ranch in Calgary. OPPOSITE: In Washington, after visiting the President and Mrs. Roosevelt at the White House, in the summer of 1942.

Two informal portraits made in the Bahamas. OVERLEAF: The Duke enjoying a favorite sport.

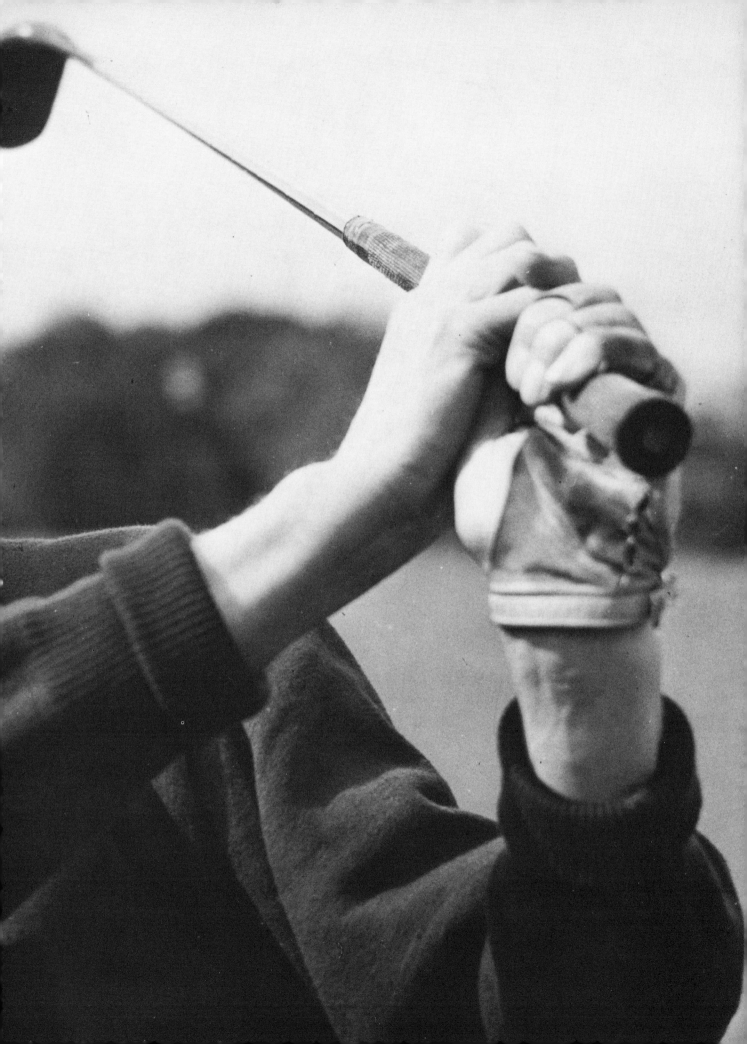

ABOVE: Aboard the *Queen Mary* on one of their frequent transatlantic crossings. OPPOSITE: The Duchess during their visit to England in 1947.

In the autumn of 1945 the Duke and Duchess returned to Paris. Anxious for another job, in fulfilment of his final broadcast offer to serve his country in any private capacity, he paid several visits to Britain. But no job materialized. He thus settled with the Duchess in France where, after an eight-year search, they eventually found a permanent home—to be exact, two homes, one in Paris, the other in the country outside it. At last, at the age of sixty, the Duke could collect and unpack his possessions and furniture, which had lain in storage at Frogmore, near Windsor, for twenty years. At last, with the aid of his wife, he could create around him the domestic conjugal environment that a man needs in middle age and that he had craved since he gave up his throne for it.

A round of parties. ABOVE: Dancing in New York. RIGHT: The Duchess and Gertrude Lawrence. OVERLEAF: The Duchess wears a carnival mask; at another ball she and the Duke exchange a few words with the ex-King and Queen of Yugoslavia.

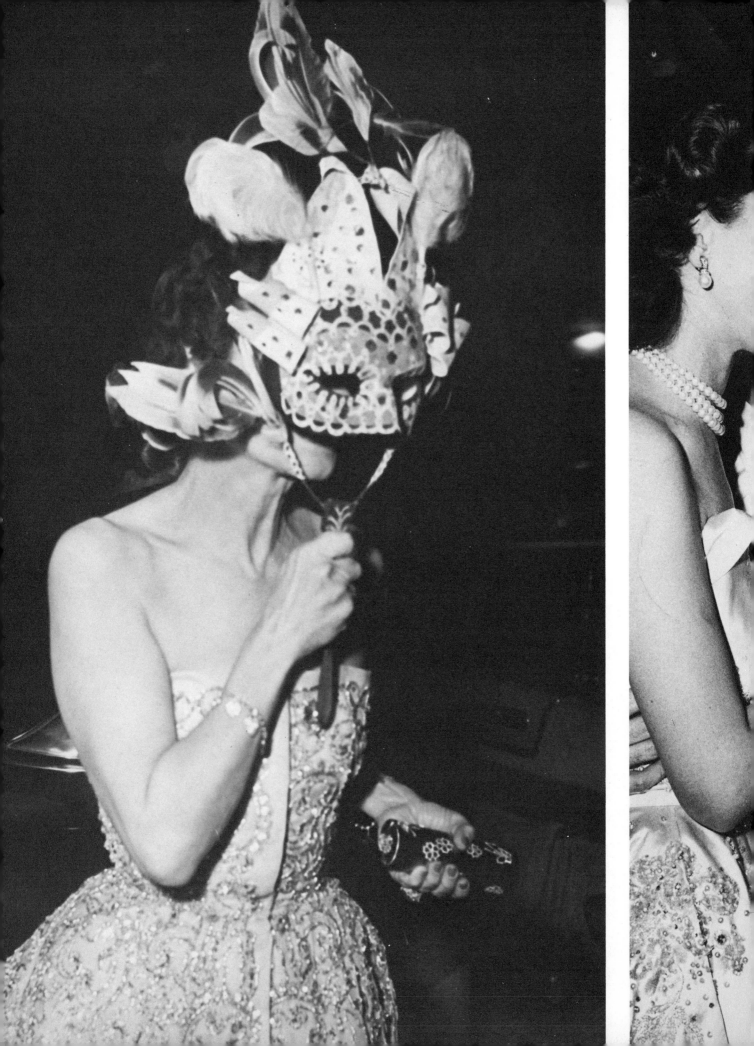

In 1947, the biggest social event in England, which was not attended by the Duke and Duchess, was the wedding of the Duke's niece, Princess Elizabeth, to the Duke of Edinburgh, on November 20. The photograph shows: (Front row, left to right) Lady Milford Haven, Princess Alice of Greece, Princess Margaret, Prince William of Gloucester (side-face), Marquess of Milford Haven, Princess Elizabeth, the Duke of Edinburgh, Prince Michael of Kent, Princess Alexandra of Kent, the King, the Queen, the Duke of Gloucester, Prince Richard of Gloucester, Duchess of Gloucester, Princess René of Bourbon Parma, Princess Marie Louise, Crown Prince of Sweden (extreme right), and Princess Helena Victoria (seated). (Middle row) Prince George of Denmark, Princess Marie of Greece, Countess Mountbatten, the Duchess of Kent, Princess Juliana of the Netherlands, Queen Frederika of the Hellenes, Queen Mary, Queen Victoria Eugenia of Spain, Queen Ingrid of Denmark, Crown Princess of Sweden, Duchess of Aosta, Princess Eugénie of Greece. (Back row) King Peter of Yugoslavia, Queen Alexandra of Yugoslavia (hidden), Earl Mountbatten of Burma, Count of Barcelona (half-hidden), Prince Bernhardt of the Netherlands, King Haakon of Norway, Prince George of Greece, Prince René of Bourbon Parma, King Frederick of Denmark, King Michael of Rumania, Prince Michel of Bourbon Parma, Princess Elizabeth of Luxembourg (partly hidden), Prince John of Luxembourg (partly hidden).

The Duke during one of his last visits to his mother.

Queen Mary holds Prince Charles, Elizabeth's first child (now heir to the throne), on his christening day. Prince Charles was born on November 14, 1948.

The Duke continued periodically to visit his country. Without the Duchess he attended successively the funerals of his brother King George VI, who had died at the untimely age of fifty-six, and of his mother Queen Mary, who died a year later at the riper age of eighty-five. He did not attend the coronation of his niece, Queen Elizabeth II. With the Duchess he came annually

On February 6, 1952, King George VI died at Sandringham. ABOVE: Crowds in London read the news in the evening paper. OPPOSITE: With bent head, Elizabeth (now Queen Elizabeth II) stands at the grave of her father after his coffin has been lowered through the floor in St. George's Chapel, Windsor Castle. The Duke of Windsor stands behind the veiled figures of his mother, sister-in-law (widow of the dead king), and Princess Margaret. Also seen in the first row center, at the far right of him, are the Duke of Gloucester and the Duke of Edinburgh.

to London, where, scrupulous in his resolve to avoid embarrassment to the Crown, he refrained from public activities and studiously avoided the limelight. He spent a part of each year in America, where the limelight was often less easy to avoid.

As Duff Cooper once sagely remarked to the Duchess, "You and the Duke have none of the advantages of royalty and all its disadvantages." They could not help attracting public attention, wherever they went. Yet they could not, as reigning royalty does, use the advantages of organized public relations to

The Duke raises his hand in sad farewell as he leaves London.

A year after the death of King George VI, sorrowing crowds again line Whitehall as Queen Mary's coffin is taken on a gun carriage for her Lying-in-State in Westminster Hall. The royal dukes march past the Cenotaph.

redress press distortions. Thus there emerged a false image of their private life, as that of a rootless, gregarious couple, given to trivial social pursuits. In the eyes of his disillusioned admirers Prince Charming, the popular hero deposed from his pedestal, assumed all too easily the guise of the playboy who would not grow up. Ill-wishers spread rumours that the Duke and Duchess of Windsor were dissatisfied not merely with their existence but with one another. The true picture of the ex-King's life in exile failed to emerge.

The coronation of Elizabeth II on June 2, 1953. ABOVE: The Queen, wearing St. Edward's crown and holding the Royal Sceptre and the Rod with the Dove, sits on the Throne as she prepares to receive homage. On her right is the Archbishop of York, Dr. Ramsay. OPPOSITE: The Queen leaves Westminster Abbey, wearing the Imperial State Crown, for her return to Buckingham Palace in the Royal Coach.

The Duke of Windsor at Antibes with Mr. and Mrs. Winston Churchill. ABOVE: With the Duchess at Portofino.

His image bears comparison with that of many another Englishman in retirement, endowed with discriminating tastes and ample private means. Its setting is first the house in town, an urban villa in the traditional French style in the Bois de Boulogne, standing amid spacious lawns and trees, with a lamp-post imported from London to light the drive, and a notice at its entrance: SMALL DOGS. PLEASE DRIVE SLOWLY. The dogs are the retired Englishman's pets, five stalwart and unruly pugs, effigies of whose eighteenth-century forebears, in porcelain, embellish the drawing-room within.

The Duke chatting with Mrs. John F. Kennedy and (OVERLEAF) with
Senator Kennedy in New York.

The Duchess with Elsa Maxwell in 1959.

In the living room of their house in the Bois de Boulogne, with their pugs, Disraeli and Davy Crockett. ABOVE: The exterior.

Here the furnishing combines the elegance of the French style with the comfort of the English. On the walls hang portraits by Royal Academicians of Queen Mary and the Duke himself as Prince of Wales. Adjoining is a small library, with deep arm-chairs and an Aubusson carpet, surrounded by shelves where the Duke has arranged his collection of leather-bound books, many of them signed by the authors—a library of the times through which he has lived. Here the Duke and Duchess entertain discriminately and informally, giving dinners—seldom luncheons, never cocktail parties—to more friends than acquaintances, among them many Americans, and providing them, in the true royal tradition, with food and drink and service of a superlative quality.

But the Duke's true love is his old mill-house and garden in the secluded Chevreuse valley. For he is by nature a countryman, while his wife is by inclination a townswoman. To The Mill guests come at weekends to enjoy a free-and-easy atmosphere which the French see as essentially English—as English as the Duke's own Churchillian French accent. The guests are housed comfortably in separate stone-flagged, timbered out-buildings, converted into self-contained "cottages."

They relax in a large living-room, formerly a barn and now adorned with relics of the Duke's career which are in fact relics of English history. Notable among them, beneath regimental banners draped from the rafters and beside drums of the Brigade of Guards converted into coffee tables, stands the Chippendale table, suitably inscribed, on which King Edward VIII signed the Instrument of Abdication in 1936.

In The Mill the Duke has found a successor to Fort Belvedere. Around it, where a stream meanders through meadows and among willow-trees, he has created an English garden—a *jardin anglais,* which his French friends admire

291

and, in a growing anglophile spirit, seek to emulate. Within its walls are herbaceous borders and lawns; beyond them a water-garden and a rock-garden such as he made at The Fort, with a waterfall ingeniously contrived to tumble down over the rocks and among the trees of the opposite hillside.

Throughout his life the Duke has devoted much of his energy to sport: in youth to hunting, in middle age to golf. In later years he turned rather to the less exacting but equally absorbing pastime of gardening. No mere planner and overseer, he prided himself, here at The Mill as at The Fort, on being, as he put it, a "dirt gardener," putting on rubber boots and corduroys, taking up trowel and secateurs to work among the men he employed.

All his life, first as Prince of Wales, then as King, then as Governor of the Bahamas, the Duke of Windsor has had work to do. "I never take things easy," he says. "I never have done." He is by nature and training a man of action, a man of energy; but he is also a man of resource and resilience, not easily bored with life. Thus he has learnt through these years how to direct his interests into leisured pursuits. He takes a keen interest in public affairs, reading all the newspapers each morning and expressing strong personal opinions on the news. He interests himself, as befits a man of means, in his own financial affairs, following the stock markets, planning his investments, keeping in daily touch with his stockbroker. When, to his disappointment, his country could no longer employ him, he was offered private jobs, in commerce and industry. But to avoid compromising the Royal Family, he consistently refused them. Instead, he set to work on his memoirs, *A King's Story,* which ranks as a notable contribution to English contemporary history and which was to serve as the basis of a film on his life. Together with two subsequent books, it throws sidelights on this period which will interest future generations in the manner of Queen Victoria's *Letters* and the *Journal of My Life in the Highlands.* These works, together with the Duchess's memoirs, *The Heart Has Its Reasons,* have served to offset the travesties of other writers and, without in any way embarrassing his family, to set their record straight for posterity.

This monarch in retirement is entirely sincere when he says, "I have found a contentment I never knew before." Boyish still in spirit, for all his years; youthful still in figure, thanks to a careful regard for his weight; informal in his manners, frank and humorous in his talk, the Duke of Windsor retains that natural zest for life in its various aspects familiar in the Prince of Wales. The basic explanation is simple enough. He is happily married to the woman he loves.

Few modern marriages have stood the test of time better than that of the

In his library in Paris. Reflected in the mirror is the face of the author, Lord Kinross.

Duke and Duchess of Windsor. In character they complement each other. The Duchess is a strong personality, with a competent executive streak in her nature. She is a paragon among housekeepers, maintaining in the houses she runs for her husband the highest standard of comfort and taste. She is an expert on interior decoration. She has a flair for entertaining, disguising an inherent shyness to put guests at their ease, to keep them amused—and amusing. She diffuses gaiety, vitality, and wit. She dresses simply and elegantly, more than holding her own in a city where the conception of *chic* reigns supreme over society. She has the slim figure of a far younger woman.

Outwardly she may sometimes appear to be the dominant partner in the marriage. In fact she is not. The Duke defers to her in matters concerned with the house and their social activities. But he is a man of strong will, as his actions have shown, a man determined to have his own way. There is within him an aloof force, a hidden dimension which his wife respects and which she has defined as the "inner essence of royalty."

Perhaps it is less easily definable. But at least it serves to balance and to harmonize a human relationship, between two positive characters, which has endured through a generation of stresses and strains. Here is a marriage based on loving companionship and close understanding.

When *A King's Story* was published in London the Duke recorded a broadcast (never delivered on account of his brother's illness) which summed up his feelings concerning it:

> While *A King's Story* is strictly non-fiction, I do believe that as far as its last chapters are concerned it is in a personal sense a romance; and speaking for the lovely and wonderful lady to whom this book is dedicated and for myself, I only wish that I had thought to add the old familiar ending to all romances, "And they lived happily ever after." And although we live abroad I always remember with pride that Britain is my native land. Your land and mine.

Only one cloud lingered from the storm of the abdication to cast over his life a perceptible shadow of sadness. All should now have been serene. For the monarchy, the ending had been a happy one too. King George VI, with his undeviating spirit of dedication to the Crown, and the "matchless blessing," as his brother had put it, of a wife and family staunchly behind him, built up the monarchy throughout the war and into the difficult period of social evolution which followed it, to new heights of prestige and security, such as it had seldom known before. And there it stands under his daughter, Queen Elizabeth, today. Far from losing by the abdication the country had gained by it. All in the end had turned out for the best. The bulk of the British people now felt only goodwill towards a man who had given so much of his youth to his country, and towards the woman who had given him happiness.

Yet the Duke of Windsor and his Duchess remained in exile from his family circle. Still the Duchess had not been received, even unofficially, by any member of the Royal Family. Still the two of them were not entitled, in his words, "to use the same front door."

On her visit to the Duke in 1965, the Queen met the Duchess for the first time since their marriage.

But in the winter of 1964 the Duke, who had now reached the age of seventy, fell suddenly ill, and was obliged to undergo a major operation in a hospital in Houston, Texas. A few months later he was threatened with the loss of the sight of one eye, and underwent three operations in London, which ultimately saved it. While he was convalescing in the London Clinic, Queen Elizabeth paid two visits to her uncle, whom she had not seen since childhood. And, for the first time since his marriage, she met and greeted the Duchess.

Thus, after twenty-eight years, bygones were allowed to become bygones. The Duke of Windsor was reunited with his family circle in the company of the

OVERLEAF: On holiday in Spain.

woman for whom he had given up his throne. In May 1967 the Queen invited the Duke and Duchess to attend the unveiling of a plaque in memory of Queen Mary at Marlborough House in London. This event enabled the Duchess to meet many of the English royal family for the first time. And so a stormy chapter of English history was finally and happily closed.

(*The text by the late Lord Kinross was written in 1967.*)

OPPOSITE AND ABOVE: Members of the royal party, after the dedication of the plaque to the memory of Queen Mary at Marlborough House on June 7, 1967. Embraces and smiles were exchanged as the Duke and Duchess chatted with the Duke's sister-in-law, the Queen Mother Elizabeth, and (ABOVE) with his niece, Queen Elizabeth II. Queen Mary, who died in 1953, moved to Marlborough House after her husband, George V, died and their son, the present Duke of Windsor, became King.

INDEX

In the garden at the mill in France.